BIKING MISSOURI'S RAIL-TRAILS

OTHER BOOKS BY
SHAWN E. RICHARDSON

Biking Ohio's Rail-Trails
Biking Wisconsin's Rail-Trails

BIKING MISSOURI'S RAIL-TRAILS

Where to Go • What to Expect • How to Get There

by
SHAWN E. RICHARDSON

ADVENTURE PUBLICATIONS, INC.
Cambridge, MN

ADVENTURE PUBLICATIONS, INC.
P.O. Box 269
Cambridge, MN 55008
1-800-678-7006

BIKING MISSOURI'S RAIL-TRAILS
Where to Go, What to Expect, How to Get There

First Printing 1999

ISBN 1-885061-59-5

Text, research, Cartography, and Photography by Shawn E. Richardson. Additional photography by David Bradford, Nick Decker, Deborah Markman, Tom Nagel, Terry Whaley, The Ozark Greenways Inc., and the Missouri Department of Natural Resources.

Edited by Tony Dierckins

Cover and Interior design by Jonathan A. Norberg

Front cover:
   Central photo: The Katy Trail State Park, Missouri (MO-DNR, Nick Decker).
   Inset photo: Rocheport Tunnel along the Katy Trail State Park (Shawn E. Richardson).
Back cover:
   Top: The former St. Charles Depot along the Katy Trail State Park.
   Middle: Inside Rocheport Tunnel along the Katy Trail State Park.
   Bottom: Watkins Mill State Park Bike Path (MO-DNR, Tom Nagel).

Special thanks to Deborah A. Schnack, Wallace Keck, Larry Larson, B.H. Rucker, and the many other folks with the Missouri Department of Natural Resources for assisting me with the research and photographs of Missouri's State Parks. Thanks also to Kevin Keach of Trailnet Inc. and Terry Whaley of the Ozark Greenways for providing me with current trail network information. And as always, special thanks to the Rails-to-Trails Conservancy and all the recreationalists who use these trails.

Most of all, I would like to thank Kevin Keach, Terry Whaley, and my wife Joyce A. Richardson, for joining me in adventuring across Missouri's rail-trails.

CONTENTS

INTRODUCTION

I researched and created Biking Missouri's Rail-Trails as a guide to Missouri's major off-road multipurpose trails and rail-trails. The book is designed to provide tourists, weekend travelers, outdoor enthusiasts, and recreationalists with a set of uniform, detailed maps that allow them to easily find each trail. The maps and text also help drivers find parking and other locations to drop off or pick up trail users. Maps of trails with permanent mile markers help users calculate the distance of their outdoor excursions.

The trails described herein have a smooth surface to allow users to bicycle, mountain bicycle, walk, hike, or travel by wheelchair. Many are open to cross-country skiers during the winter months and some even allow horseback riding. Best of all, Missouri prohibits motorized vehicles from using the trails at any time, providing a safe alternative to non-motorized users throughout the year. Check each individual trail to make sure it allows for your intended use.

The maps and information in Biking Missouri's Rail-Trails are current as of 1999. Future editions will include trails currently under development, a list of which appears under "Missouri's Potential Rail-Trails" on page 68. If you find that any of the maps need corrections, or if you have discovered trails not listed, write to me in care of Biking USA's Rail-Trails, P.O. Box 284, Hilliard, OH 43026-0284. I hope this book makes bicycling across the Show Me state more convenient and enjoyable for you, and whenever you use these paths, always keep in mind the safety tips listed in the back of this book. Happy Trails!

— Shawn E. Richardson, 1999

THE RAILS-TO-TRAILS CONSERVANCY

Founded in 1985 with the mission of enhancing America's communities and countryside, the Rails-to-Trails Conservancy is a national nonprofit organization dedicated to converting abandoned rail corridors into a nationwide network of multipurpose trails. By linking parks, schools, neighborhoods, communities, towns, cities, states, and national parks, this system will connect important landmarks and create both a haven for wildlife and a safe place for able and handicapped adults and children to bicycle, walk, in-line skate, and travel by wheelchair. Rail-trails meet demands for local recreational opportunities and connect with long-distance trails to make it possible to ride continuously across a state and eventually from coast to coast without encountering a motorized vehicle.

This vision of the Rails-to-Trails Conservancy is quickly becoming a reality. Over 1,000 trails totaling more than 10,000 miles have already been successfully converted into multipurpose trails in the United States, and over another 1,000 rail-trails are in the works.

Since the opening of the first 4.7-mile section of the M.K.T. Nature/Fitness Trail (Missouri's first rail-trail) during 1983, Missouri's rail-trail network today has grown to seven trails totalling 291 miles. The trail network continues to grow, and Missouri is connecting its trails to most of its bordering states. Grassroots efforts are taking place throughout Missouri to convert even more miles of abandoned railroads into scenic greenways.

Your membership, support, and enthusiasm will help the Rails-to-Trails Conservancy as well as the state of Missouri continue to make their vision become a reality. See page 80 for information on how you can join the Rails-to-Trails Conservancy.

MISSOURI DEPARTMENT OF NATURAL RESOURCES

The Missouri Department of Natural Resources acquires rail corridors and transforms them into smooth-surfaced bicycle trails. It takes about as much effort to remove the rails and ties as it did to build the railroads over a century ago. After the rails and ties are removed, bridges are planked, guard rails are erected, crushed limestone is laid and graded, and safety directional signs and mile markers are installed. There are ongoing costs to maintain the smooth trail surfaces, bridges, and signs and to pick up litter and debris.

In addition to the shorter state park bike paths, the Missouri DNR is known for the 235-mile Katy Trail State Park, converted from the former Katy Railroad which parallels a 164-mile section of the Missouri River.

For more information on Missouri's state parks, forests, and trails, or to request campground reservation forms, call or write:

Missouri Department of Natural Resources
P.O. Box 176, Jefferson, MO 65102
800-334-6946; 800-379-2419 (TDD)
http://www.katytrail.showmestate.com

TRAILNET INC. (ST. LOUIS AREA)

Trailnet Incorporated's mission is to develop multi-use trails, conserve greenways, and encourage walking and bicycling for recreation and transportation in the St. Louis metropolitan region. Converting abandoned railroad right-of-ways into scenic trails is a high priority. Covering the St. Louis metropolitan region of Missouri and Illinois, Trailnet Inc. researches and plans an interconnected network of multi-purpose trails, advocates trails and greenways on local and state levels, purchases and develops abandoned rail corridors, and raises funds for land conservation. Trailnet Inc. has been involved in constructing the St. Louis Riverfront Trail, Grant's Trail, West Alton Trail, and the Route 66 Bikeway. For more information, call or write:

Trailnet Inc.
3900 Reavis Barracks Rd.
St. Louis, MO 63125
314-416-9930
http://www.trailnet.org

OZARK GREENWAYS INC. (SPRINGFIELD AREA)

Ozark Greenways aquires and preserves greenways in the Springfield area, mostly through the efforts of concerned private citizens. Many volunteers and members work together to contribute to the development and promotion of greenways in Springfield. Ozark Greenways Inc., a private not-for-profit organization, has been involved in constructing the Frisco Highline Trail, the South Creek/Wilson Creek Greenway, and the Galloway Creek Greenway. For more information, call or write:

Ozark Greenways
P.O. Box 50733
Springfield, MO 65805
417-864-2014
http://www.springfield.missouri.org/gov/ozarkgreenways

TRAIL DESCRIPTIONS

ASPHALT OR CONCRETE — suitable for biking, mountain bicycling, hiking, in-line skating, and wheelchairs.

COARSE ASPHALT — suitable for bicycling, mountain bicycling, hiking, and wheelchairs.

SMOOTH CRUSHED GRAVEL — suitable for bicycling, mountain bicycling, hiking, and wheelchairs. During thawing and extremely wet weather, bicycles, mountain bicycles, and wheelchairs should avoid using this trail surface because the soft surface can rut easily.

COARSE CRUSHED GRAVEL — suitable for mountain bicycling and hiking.

GRASS OR DIRT — suitable for mountain biking and hiking.

ORIGINAL BALLAST — difficult for most trail users due to the size of larger rocks.

NOTE: Trail users should check conditions for each trail by contacting the trail managers listed in this book.

LEGEND

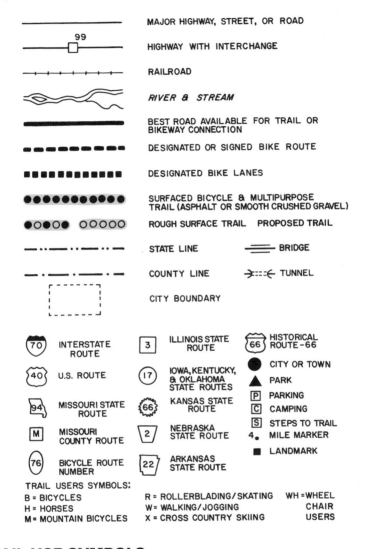

————————	MAJOR HIGHWAY, STREET, OR ROAD
——⟦99⟧———	HIGHWAY WITH INTERCHANGE
—+—+—+—+—+—	RAILROAD
≈≈≈≈≈≈≈≈	*RIVER & STREAM*
▬▬▬▬▬▬▬▬	BEST ROAD AVAILABLE FOR TRAIL OR BIKEWAY CONNECTION
■ ■ ■ ■ ■ ■ ■	DESIGNATED OR SIGNED BIKE ROUTE
■■■■■■■■■	DESIGNATED BIKE LANES
●●●●●●●●●●	SURFACED BICYCLE & MULTIPURPOSE TRAIL (ASPHALT OR SMOOTH CRUSHED GRAVEL)
●○●○● ○○○○○	ROUGH SURFACE TRAIL PROPOSED TRAIL
—··—··—··—	STATE LINE
—·—·—·—·—	COUNTY LINE
⌐ ¬ (dashed box)	CITY BOUNDARY

BRIDGE

TUNNEL

(70) INTERSTATE ROUTE	[3] ILLINOIS STATE ROUTE	(66) HISTORICAL ROUTE-66
(40) U.S. ROUTE	(17) IOWA, KENTUCKY, & OKLAHOMA STATE ROUTES	● CITY OR TOWN
		▲ PARK
(94) MISSOURI STATE ROUTE	(66) KANSAS STATE ROUTE	P PARKING
		C CAMPING
[M] MISSOURI COUNTY ROUTE	(2) NEBRASKA STATE ROUTE	S STEPS TO TRAIL
		4● MILE MARKER
(76) BICYCLE ROUTE NUMBER	⟨22⟩ ARKANSAS STATE ROUTE	■ LANDMARK

TRAIL USERS SYMBOLS:
B = BICYCLES
H = HORSES
M = MOUNTAIN BICYCLES

R = ROLLERBLADING/SKATING
W = WALKING/JOGGING
X = CROSS COUNTRY SKIING

WH = WHEEL
CHAIR
USERS

TRAIL USE SYMBOLS

Dark symbols: trail use allowed. Light symbols: trail use not allowed

🚲 Bicycling   🚵 Mountain Bicycling

🚶 Hiking   🛼 In-line Skating

🏇 Bridal Path   ⛷ Cross-Country Skiing

♿ Handicap Accessible

STATE MAP SHOWING MISSOURI'S TRAILS

MAJOR TRAIL MAP IN BOOK

© 1998

LEGEND

RT: MAJOR RAIL-TRAIL
(greater than 1 mile and/or smooth surface trail following a former railroad)

BT: BIKE TRAIL
(smooth trail that does not follow a former railroad)

MISSOURI'S TRAILS

TRAIL NAME	VICINITY	MAP CODE	PAGE#
Babler (Dr. Edmund A.) Memorial State Park Bike Path	St. Louis	BT-7	62
Forest Park Bike Path	St. Louis	BT-3	52
Frisco Greenway Trail	Joplin	RT-3	34
Frisco Highline Trail	Springfield	RT-7	42
Galloway Creek Greenway	Springfield	BT-6	60
Grant's Trail	St. Louis	RT-4	36
Jefferson City Greenway	Jefferson City	RT-6	40
Katy Trail State Park	Clinton/ JeffersonCity/ St. Louis	RT-2	4
M.K.T. Nature/Fitness Trail	Columbia	RT-1	2
Route 66 Bikeway	St. Louis	BT-5	58
St. Joe State Park Bike Path	De Lassus	BT-2	50
St. Joseph Bike Path	St. Joseph	BT-8	64
St. Louis Riverfront Trail	St. Louis	BT-5	56
South Creek/Wilson Creek Greenway	Springfield	BT-6	60
Watkins Mill State Park Bike Path	Lawson	BT-1	48
West Alton Trail	West Alton, MO/ Alton, IL	RT-5	38
Weston Bend State Park Bike Path	Weston	BT-4	54

MISSOURI'S MAJOR RAIL-TRAILS

M. K. T. NATURE/FITNESS TRAIL

VICINITY: *Columbia*

TRAIL LENGTH: *8.9 miles*

SURFACE: *Smooth crushed gravel*

TRAIL USE:

Constructed in 1983 as Missouri's first rail-trail, the M.K.T. Nature/Fitness Trail initially ran 4.7 miles between Cherry Street near the center of Columbia and the University of Missouri to Scott Boulevard on the Southwest end of Columbia. The trail takes its name from the former Missouri-Kansas-Texas Railroad (M.K.T.). In the mid 1990s, the cross-state Katy Trail State Park was constructed 4.2 miles away from the M.K.T. Nature/Fitness Trail. With the gap that was bridged in 1996 between Scott Boulevard in Columbia and the Katy Trail State Park in McBaine, the M.K.T. Nature/Fitness Trail grew to 8.9 miles.

Milepost 0 sits at the center of Columbia and the University of Missouri campus. Between mileposts 3 and 4, the trail winds through the Forum Nature Area, which has walking trails separate from the M.K.T Trail. Near milepost 4 riders can enjoy the Hinkson Woods Natural History Area, a wooded floodplains untouched by development. Brushwood Lake sits in the middle of a beautiful wetland area between mileposts 6 and 7. An occassional flood between mileposts 7 and 8 creates a rougher trail surface (improvements are planned along this section of the trail). The M.K.T. Nature/Fitness Trail intersects with the Katy Trail State Park at milepost 8.9, about a quarter mile from the town of McBaine.

PARKING:

Parking can be found in Columbia along Stadium Boulevard, Forum Boulevard, and Scott Boulevard; parking is also available along County Route K in McBaine.

People of all ages enjoy the M.K.T. Nature/Fitness Trail.

FOR MORE INFORMATION:
City of Columbia Parks and Recreation Dept.
P.O. Box N, Columbia, MO 65205
573-874-7204

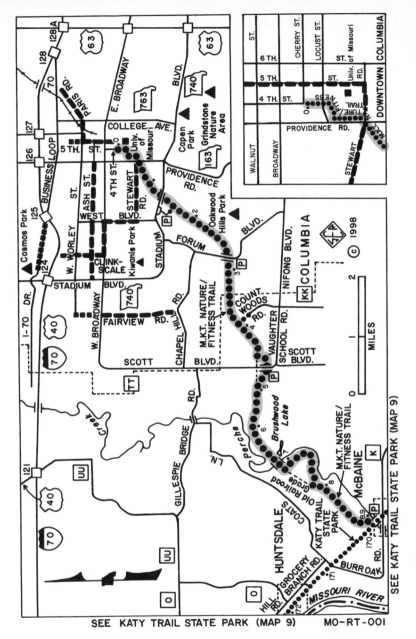

M.K.T. NATURE/FITNESS TRAIL
BOONE COUNTY
8.9 MILES
SURFACE: SMOOTH CRUSHED GRAVEL

SEE KATY TRAIL STATE PARK (MAP 9)   MO-RT-001

3

KATY TRAIL STATE PARK

VICINITY: *St. Louis, Jefferson City, and Clinton*
TRAIL LENGTH: *235 miles*
SURFACE: *Smooth crushed gravel*
TRAIL USE: 🚲 🚵 🚶 📷 🏇 ⛷ ♿

The Katy Trail State Park offers a unique opportunity for cross-country cyclists. The trail's 235-miles provide cyclists many recreational options in a natural setting as they discover the past along a former railroad line. The Katy Trail State Park follows the former M.K.T. Railroad, also known as the Katy Railroad. When a 200-mile section of the Katy Railroad between Machens and Sedalia was abandoned in 1986, Edward D. (Ted) Jones recognized the rare opportunity to create Missouri's second rail-trail. This trail winds its way through the Missouri River Valley, rich with history and full of natural beauty. Jones' generosity made it possible to purchase the 200-mile corridor from the railroad, and he spent time earning support from local citizens and the Missouri Department of Natural Resources. In 1991, the railroad donated an additional 33 miles of rail corridor between Sedalia and Clinton.

In March of 1990, the first 5-mile section of the Katy Trail opened in Rocheport. During the early 1990s, other sections running from St. Charles to Marthasville and from Jefferson City to Booneville opened to the public. Two major floods in 1993 and 1995 destroyed many sections of the Katy Trail, but repairs were implemented by the end of 1996; that same year, the trail was completed from St. Charles to Sedalia. In 1998, another 33 miles of the trail opened between Sedalia and Clinton. In the near future, the last 11-mile section will open between Machens and St. Charles, making the entire rail-trail a continuous 235 miles.

The trail allows users to travel through some of the most scenic areas of the state. The majority of the trail closely follows the Missouri River, whose bluffs tower along both banks. The trail runs through many different landscapes, including dense forests, wetlands, deep valleys, open pastureland, and gently rolling farm fields. Wildflowers color the trail during various blooming seasons, and birdwatchers will delight in the variety of avian wildlife. The Katy Trail State Park also takes users through historic rural areas as it meanders through the small towns that once flourished along the railroad corridor. The route has been designated as an official segment of the Lewis and Clark National Historic Trail between St. Charles and Boonville, and the entire Katy Trail has been designated as part of the American Discovery Trail.

The Katy Trail State Park's mile markers follow the same system used for the former railroad, and trail is marked every mile with a sign post. Donation boxes are located at trail heads along the entire Katy Trail State Park; all donations are used for trail maintenance and repairs.

The Katy Trail State Park, 235 miles long, is detailed in 14 maps.
See the map number indicated for each section of the trail.

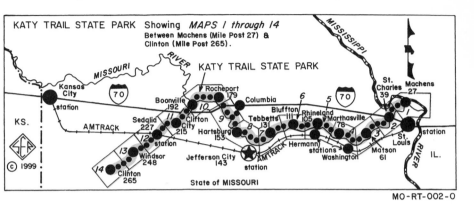

KATY TRAIL STATE PARK Showing *MAPS 1 through 14*
Between Machens (Mile Post 27) &
Clinton (Mile Post 265).

KATY TRAIL STATE PARK

MISSOURI RIVER

MISSISSIPPI

Kansas City
70
station
KS.
AMTRACK
© 1999

Rocheport 179
Boonville 192
10
Clifton City 9
Sedalia 227 11
215 Hartsburg 153
12 station
13
Windsor 248
14
Clinton 265

Columbia
Bluffton
Tebbetts 111
8 7
St. Charles 39
6 5 70
Rhineland 105 Marthasville 78
131
Hermann
stations
Jefferson City 143 AMTRACK station
Washington
Matson 61
Machens 27
1
2 St. Louis
3 station
4
IL.

State of MISSOURI

MO-RT-002-0

Katy Trail State Park (MO-DNR, Nick Decker).

5

MACHENS - ST. CHARLES *(map 1)*

The Katy Trail State Park starts in Machens (mile post 27), about 13 miles west of the confluence of the Mississippi and the Missouri Rivers, just north of St. Louis. From Machens to St. Charles, the trail goes through mostly flat farmland. Part of the trail was washed away by the flood of 1995, just northeast of St. Charles; this part of the rail-trail has been rerouted from the original railroad right-of-way.

ST. CHARLES *(map 2)*

St. Charles (mile post 39) is one of the most historic towns along the Katy Trail State Park. Its early French settlement dates back to the mid-1700s, and St. Charles was Missouri's first state capital before it was relocated to Jefferson City. The capitol building is known today as the Missouri State Capitol State Historic Site, operated by the Missouri Department of Natural Resources.

ST. CHARLES - AUGUSTA *(map 2 & 3)*

From St. Charles, the Katy Trail State Park runs southwest through the suburbs of St. Charles (between mile posts 42 and 45), Greens Bottom (between mile posts 44 and 49), and Jacobs (mile post 47). Between mile posts 51 and 55, riders pass through a thickly wooded wetland area featuring tranquil views of the Howell Island Wildlife Area. This same section of trail also offers views of the scenic stone bluffs that border the trail along the Weldon Spring Wildlife Area. The Katy Trail continues through Defiance (mile post 59), Matson (mile post 61), and Augusta (mile post 66), whose dolomite and sandstone bluffs can be seen from the trail. Augusta was settled in 1836 on the bluffs overlooking the Missouri River and is known as a center of German cultural traditions.

AUGUSTA - TRELOAR *(map 4)*

Riders can stop to visit wineries in Augusta (mile post 66), Dutzow (mile post 74) and Marthasville (mile post 78). These towns reflect the industrial age brought to this rural area by the railroad. Marthasville was established around 1800 near the site of an early French trading post dating back to 1763. Daniel Boone lived the last years of his life in this area, and his original grave site is one mile east of Marthasville (his grave was eventually relocated to Frankfort, Kentucky).

St. Charles Historical Depot (near mile post 39).

Augusta, Missouri (near mile post 66).

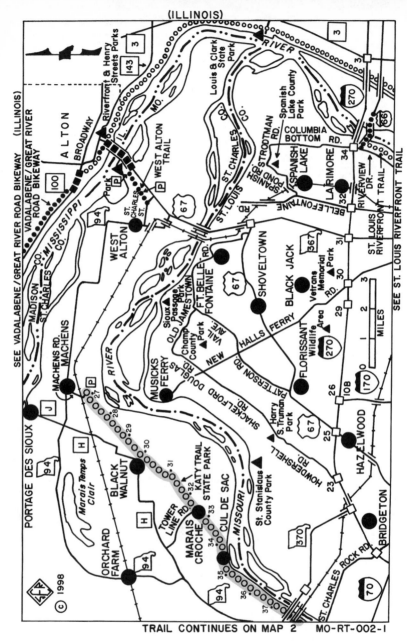

TRAIL CONTINUES ON MAP 2   MO-RT-002-1

KATY TRAIL STATE PARK (MAP 1)
ST. CHARLES, WARREN, MONTGOMERY, CALLAWAY, BOONE, HOWARD, COOPER, PETTIS, & HENRY COUNTIES
TOTAL LENGTH: 235.0 MILES
SURFACE: SMOOTH CRUSHED GRAVEL
(ASPHALT STREETS THROUGH BOONVILLE & SEDALIA)

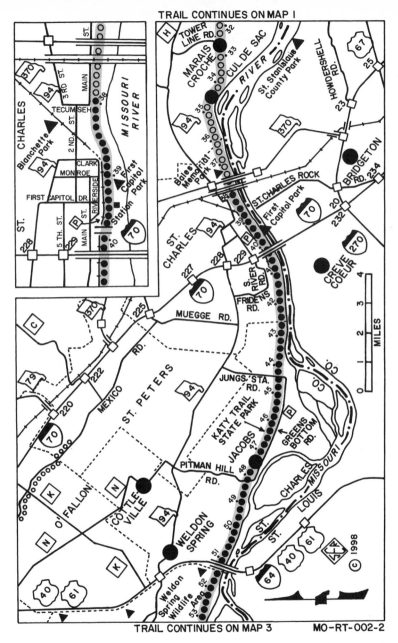

TRAIL CONTINUES ON MAP 1

TRAIL CONTINUES ON MAP 3

MO-RT-002-2

KATY TRAIL STATE PARK (MAP 2)

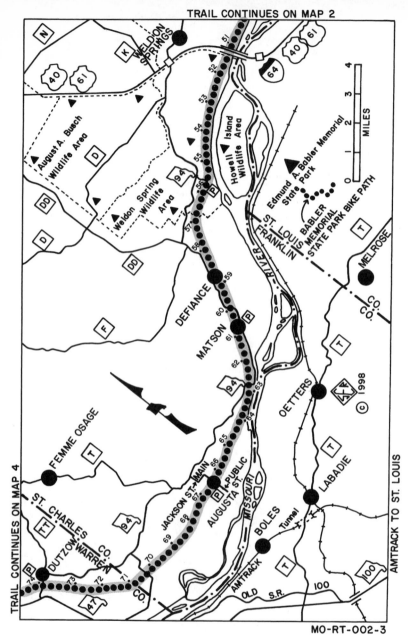

KATY TRAIL STATE PARK (MAP 3)

MO-RT-002-3

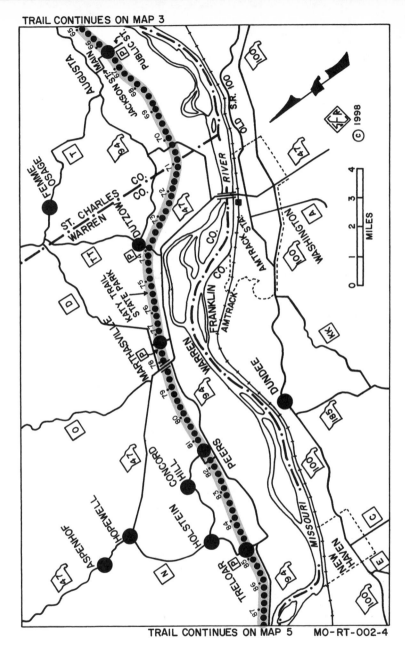

TRAIL CONTINUES ON MAP 3

TRAIL CONTINUES ON MAP 5   MO-RT-002-4

KATY TRAIL STATE PARK (MAP 4)

TRELOAR - MCKITTRICK *(map 5)*

The Katy Trail State Park continues west of Marthasville through Peers (mile post 81), Treloar (mile post 85), and Gore (mile post 94). This section of the trail passes through rural communities and farming operations. Towering 250-foot sandstone and limestone bluffs west of Treloar offer a spectacular view. Birds and a wide variety of wildflowers are found in abundance along this section of the Katy Trail State Park, which proceeds through Case (mile post 97) and McKittrick (mile post 101). Between St. Charles and Hermann (known as the "Rhineland" region), wineries and vineyards are abundant in the Missouri River Valley including throughout Dutzow, Marthasville, Defiance, and Augusta.

HERMANN *(map 5)*

If you're willing to follow State Route 19 approximately 2 miles south to the other side of the Missouri River, you can visit Hermann, which is known for it's German heritage and it's vineyards. Hermann is the home of the Deutschheim State Historic Site operated by the Department of Natural Resources. However, State Route 19 can have very heavy traffic, and even experienced bicyclists should use extreme caution.

MCKITTRICK - RHINELAND *(map 5)*

From McKittrick, the Katy Trail State Park goes west to Rhineland (mile post 105), another town steeped in German tradition. This part of the trail diverts from the original railroad right-of-way for a very short distance.

A steel railroad bridge along the Missouri River.

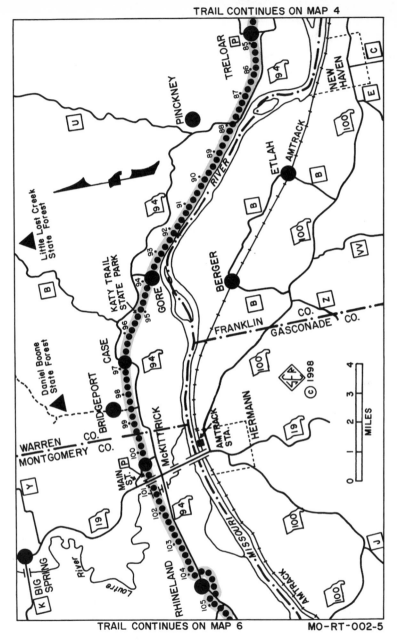

TRAIL CONTINUES ON MAP 4

TRAIL CONTINUES ON MAP 6

MO-RT-002-5

KATY TRAIL STATE PARK (MAP 5)

RHINELAND - JEFFERSON CITY *(maps 6 & 7)*

From Rhineland, the Katy Trail State Park runs slightly southwest through Bluffton (mile post 111), Portland (mile post 116), and Steedman (mile post 121). Between mile posts 111 and 117, the trail runs right next to the Missouri River, showing off several bluffs.

Rhineland, Missouri (mile post 105).

Cyclists enjoy the Katy Trail State Park.

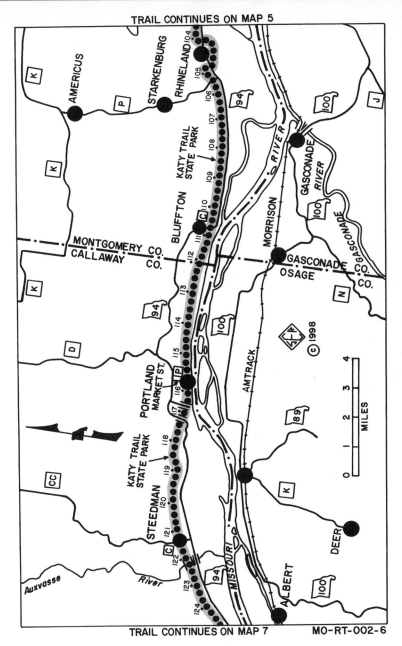

TRAIL CONTINUES ON MAP 5

TRAIL CONTINUES ON MAP 7   MO-RT-002-6

KATY TRAIL STATE PARK (MAP 6)

From Portland, the Katy Trail State Park goes southwest through Mokane (mile post 125), Tebbetts (mile post 131), and Wainwright (mile post 138). Between mile posts 117 and 142, the Katy Trail State Park follows State Route 94, straying from the Missouri River. This less scenic section of the trail passes through farmland, meadows, and spotted woodlands, but riders can see the distant bluffs and hills across the open fields and meadows along the south side of the Missouri River. Between mile posts 140 and 145 the Missouri State Capitol Building is visible on the opposite side of the Missouri River.

Many former railroad bridges like this one exist along the Katy Trail.

Jefferson City's Skyline and Missouri's State Capitol along the Missouri River (mile post 143).

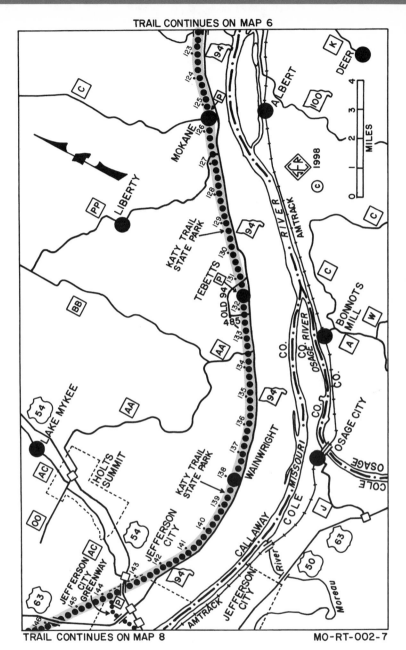

TRAIL CONTINUES ON MAP 6

TRAIL CONTINUES ON MAP 8

MO-RT-002-7

KATY TRAIL STATE PARK (MAP 7)

JEFFERSON CITY *(map 8)*

A parking lot for Jefferson City is located west of U.S. Route 54 near mile post 143. In Jefferson City, Missouri's capitol, riders can leave the Katy Trail to ride on the Jefferson City Greenway, which runs towards Jefferson City. Currently, this 1-mile trail stops just north of the Missouri River, but eventually it will extend across the Missouri River, providing trail users a safe access into the center of Jefferson City and the state capitol. At this time, it is highly recommended that cyclists do not cross the extremely dangerous U.S. Route 54 and 63 bridge. If you must cross the bridge, keep in mind that the speed limit is 70 m.p.h., the northbound bridge has a concrete shoulder, and the southbound bridge has no shoulder.

JEFFERSON CITY - EASLEY *(maps 8 & 9)*

From Jefferson City, the Katy Trail State Park goes northwest to Claysville (mile post 150) and Hartsburg (mile post 154). The scenery along this stretch consists mostly of wooded areas tucked into the bases of hillsides and bluffs. Hartsburg is a small, beautifully restored village offering bed & breakfasts, restaurants, and a bicycle shop all set inside refurbished historic buildings. From Hartsburg, the trail runs northwest to Wilton (mile post 157) and Easley (mile post 163). Between mile posts 156 and 158, the trail parallels the Missouri River.

A bed & breakfast in Hartsburg (near mile post 154).

TRAIL CONTINUES ON MAP 7

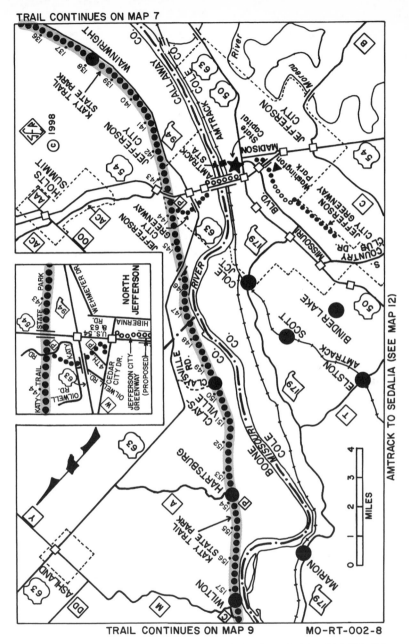

TRAIL CONTINUES ON MAP 9   MO-RT-002-8

KATY TRAIL STATE PARK (MAP 8)

19

EASLEY - ROCHEPORT *(maps 9 & 10)*

From Easley, the Katy Trail State Park runs northwest, following the Missouri River and Perche Creek to Providence (mile post 165) and McBaine (mile post 169). Between mile posts 169 and 170 near McBaine, the trail intersects with the M.K.T. Nature/Fitness Trail, an 8.9-mile rail-trail that runs to Columbia, home of three colleges including the University of Missouri. Looking toward the Missouri River near mile post 170, riders can see an extremely large tree in the far distance—the Great Burr Oak Tree of Mid-Missouri. A gravel road crossing the trail takes riders to the tree, which experts believe to be over 350 years old.

The trail proceeds northwest towards Huntsdale (mile post 172) and the Lewis and Clark Cave (between mile posts 173 and 175). A rare surviving pictograph sits above the entrance to the Lewis and Clark Cave.

Bluffs align many sections of the Katy Trail State Park.

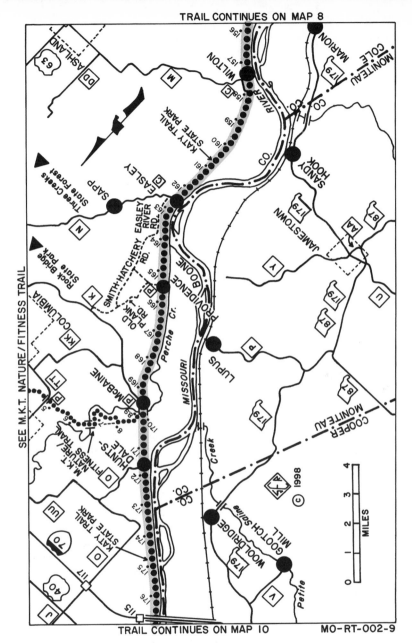

TRAIL CONTINUES ON MAP 8

TRAIL CONTINUES ON MAP 10

MO-RT-002-9

KATY TRAIL STATE PARK (MAP 9)

Between mile posts 172 and 178, the Katy Trail State Park runs right next to the Missouri River. Just below the river's high, spectacular bluffs, which Lewis and Clark mentioned in their journals of as they traveled up the Missouri River can be seen.

ROCHEPORT *(map 10)*

In Rocheport, a memorial for Edward D. (Ted) Jones, the man who made the Katy Trail dream a reality, can be found near mile post 177. Many houses found near Rocheport (mile post 178) date back before the Civil War. Today, Rocheport is a charming community offering bed & breakfasts, boutiques, wineries and specialty shops. Rocheport is also the oldest section of the Katy Trail State Park, where the first combined bicycle shop, food stop, and gift shop facility was built for trail users. Just west of Rocheport is the 243-foot long stone-arch tunnel built in 1893. This is the only railroad tunnel along the 235-mile trail.

ROCHEPORT - BOONVILLE *(map 10)*

From Rocheport, the trail goes west to New Franklin (mile post 188) and Franklin (mile post 189). In Franklin, the railroad's former round house has been turned into a campground. Between mile posts 190 and 191, is the site of Old Franklin where the Old Santa Fe Trail began; the town was washed away by a flood. From there, the Katy Trail State Park leaves the original railroad right-of-way and follows the Old State Route 87 highway grade to the U.S. Route 40 bridge. A separate path takes you across the Missouri River into the center of Boonville (mile post 191).

Rocheport Tunnel (near mile post 179).

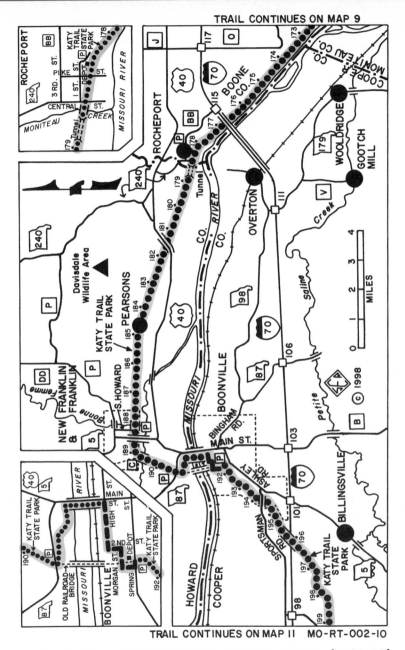

TRAIL CONTINUES ON MAP 9

TRAIL CONTINUES ON MAP 11   MO-RT-002-10

KATY TRAIL STATE PARK (MAP 10)

10

BOONVILLE *(maps 10 & 11)*

Boonville is a small river town which made the transition from a major river port to a railroad town. Founded in 1810, Boonville had a major role in both the War of 1812 and the Civil War. Today, Boonville is abundant with businesses, stores, hotels, motels, restaurants, and bed & breakfasts. Boonville has a historical society complete with folk and music festivals during certain times of the year. From here, riders follow lightly traveled back streets from the downtown area to reach the south end of town, where the rail-trail section of the Katy Trail State Park resumes (near mile post 192). Also near mile post 192, riders find the M.K.T. Depot, which has been restored by the Missouri Department of Natural Resources.

BOONVILLE - CLIFTON CITY *(maps 10 & 11)*

The landscape between mile posts 192 and 224 is more open and provides vistas across gently rolling pastures and farm land, much of which was once tallgrass prairie. Although most of the land has been converted to farm land, prairie plants can still be seen along the trail. This section of the trail winds up and down hill grades with a series of curves.

From Boonville, the Katy Trail passes through Pilot Grove (mile post 203) to Clifton City (mile post 215).

A historical building in Booneville along the Katy Trail State Park.

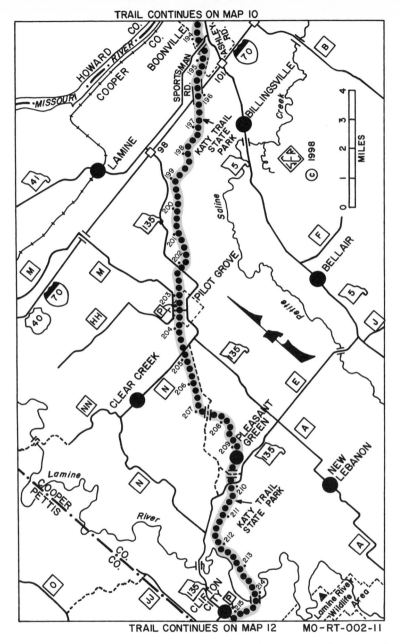

2TRAIL CONTINUES ON MAP 10

eaKaty Trail State Park • MAP 11

TRAIL CONTINUES ON MAP 12   MO-RT-002-11

KATY TRAIL STATE PARK (MAP 11)

25

From Clifton City, the trail proceeds to Sedalia (Griessen Road; mile post 224). Currently, the rail-trail ends at a parking lot. Riders take back roads posted with the Katy Trail Bike Route signs along Griessen Road, Engineer Avenue, and Third Street to enter Sedalia from the northeast.

Farmland makes most of the scenery between Boonville and Clinton.

SEDALIA *(map 12)*

Sedalia was founded in 1860 and was a wealthy business town during the railroad era. Today, Amtrack along with freight trains still come through Sedalia. Cyclists touring the Katy Trail State Park can easily start or end their bike trips from the Amtrack train station (the Amtrack station in Sedalia is different from the location of the restored M.K.T. Railroad Depot).

Sedalia is home to the Missouri State Fair. The historical M.K.T. Railroad Depot in Sedalia (mile post 227) has also been renovated for businesses. The depot was one of the largest between Kansas City and St. Louis. From the depot, the rail-trail runs southwest through the southwestern part of Sedalia to the Missouri State Fair Grounds (mile post 230).

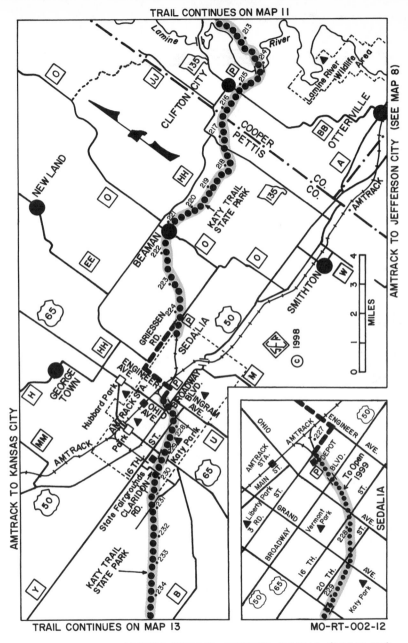

TRAIL CONTINUES ON MAP 11

TRAIL CONTINUES ON MAP 13

MO-RT-002-12

KATY TRAIL STATE PARK (MAP 12)

SEDALIA - WINDSOR *(maps 12 & 13)*

From U.S. Route 65, the Katy Trail State Park continues west past the State Fair Grounds to the towns of Green Ridge (mile post 239), Bryson (mile post 244), and Windsor (mile post 248) along gently rolling terrain surrouned by rural scenery.

In Windsor, a bicentennial M.K.T. caboose rests near the trail's parking. Windsor is home to an amish community, so bicyclists are as likely to encounter a horse drawn buggy or two. The Amish families have farms and established businesses in the city of Windsor.

The M.K.T. Bicentennial Caboose in Windsor (mile post 248).

WINDSOR - CLINTON *(maps 13 & 14)*

From Windsor, the Katy Trail State Park continues southwest to Calhoun (mile post 255) passing under State Route 52 twice. This section of the trail passes through a wooded area valley teaming with an abundance of wildlife, making it one of the most scenic sections of the Katy Trail State Park between Sedalia and Clinton. From Calhoun, the Katy Trail State Park parallels State Route 52 to Lewis (mile post 260) and Clinton (mile post 265). The scenery through here is very open and flat with ranches and portions of the prairie remain. The Katy Trail State Park currently ends on Sedalia Street in the northeast section of Clinton by the Wagoner Memorial Baseball Field and County Fair Grounds (mile post 265)

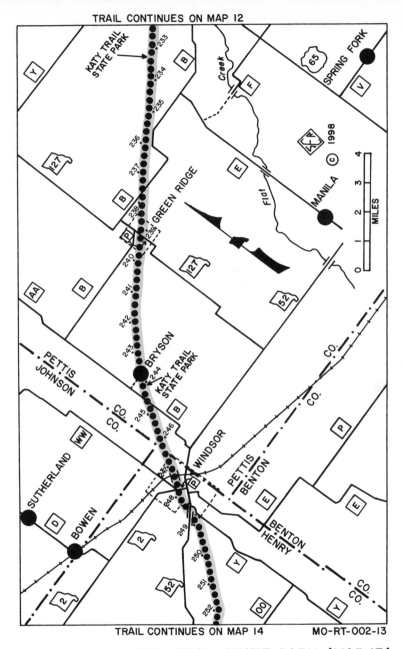

TRAIL CONTINUES ON MAP 12

KATY TRAIL STATE PARK

Y

B

Creek

F

65

SPRING FORK

V

127

E

1998

GREEN RIDGE

Flat

MANILA

4

3

2

MILES

1

0

B

P

B

127

52

AA

B

241

242

243

BRYSON

KATY TRAIL STATE PARK

CO.

PETTIS
JOHNSON

244

KATY TRAIL
STATE PARK

245

B

246

CO.
CO.

P

WW

247

WINDSOR

P

PETTIS
BENTON

SUTHERLAND

248

E

E

D

BOWEN

2

249

BENTON
HENRY

250

Y

52

2

251

CO.
CO.

2

OO

Y

252

TRAIL CONTINUES ON MAP 14   MO-RT-002-13

KATY TRAIL STATE PARK (MAP 13)

13

CLINTON *(map 14)*

Clinton is also one of the larger cities on the Katy Trail. Like Sedalia, Clinton also has a strong business community with hotels, motels, camp grounds, and restaurants. Clinton is a great spot to start or end the Katy Trail State Park journey. Currently, the M.K.T. railroad is still active into downtown Clinton. Riders can follow side streets to the beautiful, old fashioned center of town featuring the county courthouse, the Henry County Museum, and local parks. Near Clinton's old fashion town square is the Old Katy Railroad Depot; today, the depot houses the Clinton Chamber of Commerce. Future plans for the Katy Trail State Park include extending the 235-mile trail in both directions to St. Louis and Kansas City.

Katy Trail State Park, just outside Clinton.

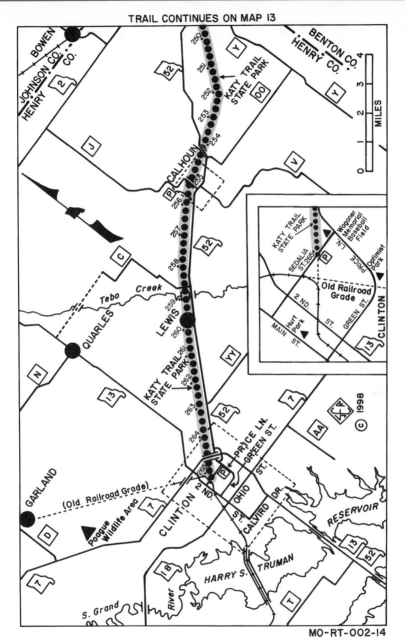

TRAIL CONTINUES ON MAP 13

MO-RT-002-14

KATY TRAIL STATE PARK (MAP 14)

AMTRACK ACROSS MISSOURI:

An Amtrack passenger train provides a bicycle shuttle service closely following the Katy Trail State Park along the south side of the Missouri River. Amtrack runs between St. Louis and Kansas City and stops in Washington, Hermann, Jefferson City, and Sedalia (see map on page 5).

For more information, call 1-800-USA-RAIL (872-7245).

HOTELS, BED & BREAKFASTS, CAMPING, RESTAURANTS, STORES, AND HISTORY:

The Katy Trail Guidebook by Brett Dufur features updated listings of where to stay, where to dine, where to shop, and what to see along the Katy Trail. A history of the Katy Railroad—along with current and historic photographs—is also included in the book, whose stories include tales of some of the folks who have lived their lives along the Katy Trail State Park, before and after the rail-to-trails conversion. For more information, call Peeble Publishing, 1-800-576-7322.

PARKING:

Parking is available along the Katy Trail State Park in the cities of Machens, St. Charles, Matson, Augusta, Dutzow, Marthasville, Treloar, McKittrick, Portland, Mokane, Tebetts, Wainwright, Jefferson City, Hartsburg, Providence, McBaine, Rocheport, New Franklin, Franklin, Boonville, Pilot Grove, Clifton City, Sedalia, Green Ridge, Windsor, Calhoun, and Clinton. Most of these parking facilities are provided by the Missouri Department of Natural Resources.

FOR MORE INFORMATION:
Missouri Dept. of Natural Resources
P.O. Box 176, Jefferson City, MO 65102
800-334-6946, 800-379-2419 (TDD)
http://www.katytrail.showmestate.com

A mileage chart has been provided showing the facilities along the Katy Trail State Park. Please note that certain facilities are scarce in many communities along the Katy Trail State Park.

AM = AMTRACK WITH BIKE SHUTTLE
B = BIKE SHOP/SERVICE/RENTAL
BB = BED & BREAKFAST
* = CITY NEAR THE KATY TRAIL STATE PARK

C = CAMPING
M = MOTEL/HOTEL/INN
R = RESTAURANT/STORE

MILE POST	CITY	CHAMBER OF COMMERCE	AM	B	BB	C	M	R
27	MACHENS							
39	ST. CHARLES	314-946-0633	AM	B	BB	C	M	R
56	WELDON SPRINGS							
59	DEFIANCE			B	BB			R
61	MATSON			B				R
66	AUGUSTA			B	BB			R
74	DUTZOW			B	BB			R
74*	WASHINGTON	314-239-2715	AM		BB		M	R
78	MARTHASVILLE			B	BB			R
81	PEERS				BB			R
84	TRELOAR			B	BB			R
101	McKITTRICK				BB			
101*	HERMANN	573-486-2313	AM	B	BB	C	M	R
105	RHINELAND							R
111	BLUFFTON			B	BB	C		
116	PORTLAND					C		R
121	STEEDMAN					C		R
125	MOKANE							R
131	TEBBETTS			B				R
138	WAINWRIGHT							
143	JEFFERSON CITY	573-634-3616	AM	B	BB	C	M	R
150	CLAYSVILLE							
154	HARTSBURG			B	BB			R
157	WILTON					C		R
163	EASLEY					C		R
166	PROVIDENCE							
170	McBAINE							R
170*	COLUMBIA	573-874-1132		B	BB	C	M	R
178	ROCHEPORT			B	BB			R
188	NEW FRANKLIN			B	BB	C		R
189	FRANKLIN					C		R
192	BOONVILLE	816-882-2721		B	BB		M	R
203	PILOT GROVE				BB			R
215	CLIFTON CITY				BB			R
227	SEDALIA	816-826-2222	AM	B	BB	C	M	R
239	GREEN RIDGE			B				R
248	WINDSOR	816-647-2318 816-647-3144			BB		M	R
255	CALHOUN							R
265	CLINTON	816-885-8168 800-222-5251		B	BB	C	M	R

FRISCO GREENWAY TRAIL

VICINITY: *Joplin*

TRAIL LENGTH: *3.8 miles*

SURFACE: *Smooth crushed Gravel*

TRAIL USE: 🚲 🚵 🚶 🛼 🐎 ⛷ ♿

The Frisco Greenway Trail, Missouri's third rails-to-trails conversion, opened in 1992. This trail follows a section of the former St. Louis & San Francisco Railroad that was donated to Jasper County by Burlington Northern. This very scenic four-mile greenway runs from Webb City to Joplin and is lined with trees, bushes, and wildflowers. Efforts are underway to extend the Frisco Greenway Trail a quarter of a mile south to connect with North Street and Railroad Avenue.

PARKING:

Parking is available on St. Louis Avenue next to the Frisco Greenway Trail.

Cyclists enjoy the Frisco Greenway Trail (Deborah Markman).

FOR MORE INFORMATION:

Joplin Trails Coalition
P.O. Box 2102, Joplin, MO 64803
417-625-3114

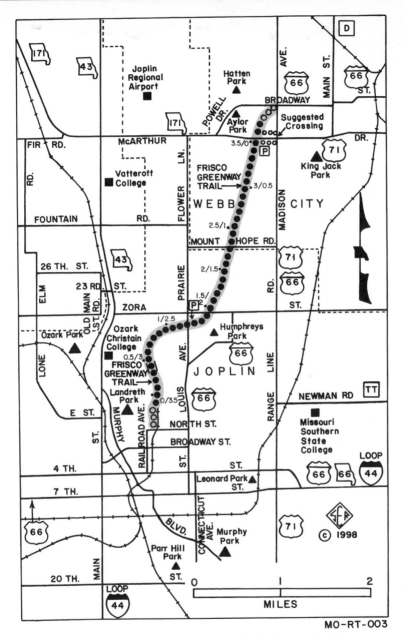

FRISCO GREENWAY TRAIL
JASPER COUNTY
3.8 MILES
SURFACE: SMOOTH CRUSHED GRAVEL

MO-RT-003

GRANT'S TRAIL

VICINITY: *St. Louis*

TRAIL LENGTH: *6.2 miles*

SURFACE: *Asphalt*

TRAIL USE: 🚲 🚴 🚶 📷 🐎 ⛷ ♿

The Grant's Trail (formerly the Carondelet Greenway Trail) opened as a rail-trail in 1994. This 6.2-mile trail, once part of the Missouri Pacific railroad line, enjoys very heavy use from bicyclists, walkers, and rollerbladers. The trail passes through the southern neighborhoods of St. Louis. It goes by an urban and suburban area adjacent to undeveloped wetlands. In 1997, the trail was renamed Grant's Trail after President Ulysses S. Grant, who established the country's first National Park. The Ulysses S. Grant National Historic Site is located in southern St. Louis County on 9.65 acres of land (between mileposts 5 and 6 of the trail). Riders can visit the Gateway Trailnet's office where Reavis Barracks Road meets the Grant's Trail (near mile post 1). The yellow brick building was formerly the Grasso Brothers Coal Company, a destination for the coal carried by the railroad's freight cars. Future plans include extending Grant's Trail west toward Sappington Road.

PARKING:

Parking can be found on Hoffmeister, Reavis Barracks Road, Union Road, and Tesshire.

Local residences enjoy a stroll along Grant's Trail.

FOR MORE INFORMATION:

Trailnet Inc.
3900 Reavis Barracks Rd.
St. Louis, MO 63125
314-416-9930 or 618-874-8554
http://www.trailnet.org

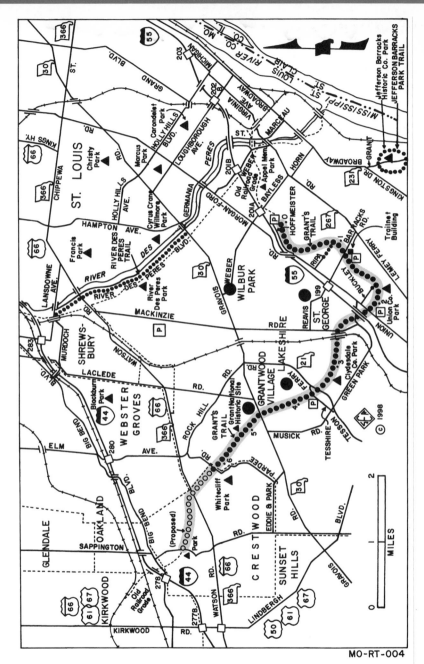

MO-RT-004

GRANT'S TRAIL
ST. LOUIS COUNTY
6.2 MILES
SURFACE: ASPHALT

WEST ALTON TRAIL

VICINITY: *West Alton, MO, and Alton, IL*

TRAIL LENGTH: *2.9 miles (1.5 mile rail-trail)*

SURFACE: *Smooth crushed gravel, asphalt, and concrete*

TRAIL USE:

The 2.9-mile West Alton Trail closely follows U.S. Route 67 from West Alton, Missouri, to Alton, Illinois. About half of the trail consists of signed bike lanes along U.S. Route 67 as it passes over the Mississippi River. The actual rail-trail is only 1.5 miles near West Alton. The West Alton Trail is 7 miles away from Machens, the beginning of the 235-mile Katy Trail State Park. In Alton, Illinois, the West Alton Trail connects to the 14-mile Vadalabene/Great River Road Bikeway. Scenery along the West Alton Trail consists of flat farmland and plenty of wetlands. Future plans include extending the trail west to Machens, where it can connect to the Katy Trail State Park.

PARKING:

Parking can be found along U.S. Route 67 northeast of St. Charles Street in West Alton. The Lincoln-Shields Recreation Area in Missouri and Ridge Street in Alton, Illinois, are more popular places to park.

Wetlands along the West Alton Trail.

FOR MORE INFORMATION:

Trailnet Inc.
3900 Reavis Barracks Rd.
St. Louis, MO 63125
314-416-9930 or 618-874-8554
http://www.trailnet.org

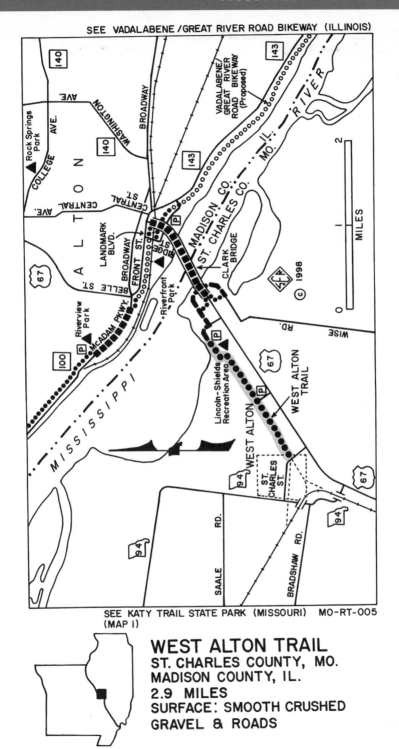

SEE VADALABENE/GREAT RIVER ROAD BIKEWAY (ILLINOIS)

WEST ALTON TRAIL
ST. CHARLES COUNTY, MO.
MADISON COUNTY, IL.
2.9 MILES
SURFACE: SMOOTH CRUSHED
GRAVEL & ROADS

SEE KATY TRAIL STATE PARK (MISSOURI)   MO-RT-005
(MAP 1)

JEFFERSON CITY GREENWAY

VICINITY: *Jefferson City*

TRAIL LENGTH: *1, 0.5, and 1.5 miles*

SURFACE: *1 mile Smooth crushed gravel; 0.5 miles Concrete; 2 miles Asphalt*

TRAIL USE:

The Jefferson City Greenway, currently under development, traverses Jefferson City. When complete, the trail network will include approximately 10 miles of riding surface. During this time, three sections of the Jefferson City Greenway are complete. The first section of the trail intersects with the Katy Trail State Park and runs one mile south to Cedar City Drive, just north of the Missouri River. The trail's second section starts on Dunklin Street, a few blocks west of the Missouri State Capitol, and runs 0.5 miles west to Washington Park. The third section of the trail follows West Edgewood Drive and Wears Creek for 2 miles between Heisinger Road and Wildwood Drive. When finished, the 10-mile Jefferson City Greenway will fully connect to the 235-mile Katy Trail State Park.

PARKING:

Parking north of the Missouri River is available on Katy Road where the Katy Trail State Park and the Jefferson City Greenway come together. Parking can also be found on Fourth Street in Cedar City.

Parking south of the Missouri River is available in Jefferson City on Dunklin Street, Kansas Street, and West Edgewood Drive.

Jefferson City's Skyline and Missouri's State Capitol along the Missouri River.

FOR MORE INFORMATION:

City of Jefferson
Dept. of Parks and Recreation
320 E. McCarty, Jefferson City, MO 65101
573-634-6482

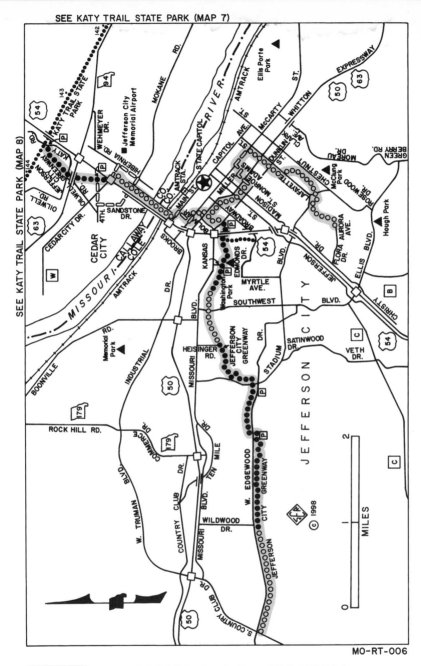

MO-RT-006

JEFFERSON CITY GREENWAY
CALLAWAY & COLE COUNTIES
1.0 MILE ; SURFACE: SMOOTH CRUSHED GRAVEL
0.5 & 2.0 MILES; ASPHALT & CONCRETE

FRISCO HIGHLINE TRAIL

VICINITY: *Springfield*

TRAIL LENGTH: *30.4 miles (10 miles open)*

SURFACE: *Smooth Crushed Gravel*

TRAIL USE: 🚲 🚵 🚶 🏕 🏇 ⛷ ♿

The Frisco Highline Trail is the first major rail-trail developed in the Ozark Region of Southwestern Missouri. Currently, only the first 10 miles of the trail, between Willard and Walnut Grove in Greene County (mile posts 183 and 173), are open for use. The mile posts along the Frisco Highline Trail follow the same numbering system used by the former Burlington Northern Railroad. This trail offers a longer trail with more open space; many cyclists from Springfield prefer the Frisco Highline Trail over the South Creek/Wilson Creek Greenway and the Galloway Creek Greenway in their own community.

The south end of the Frisco Highline Trail starts on Jackson and Miller Streets in Willard (near mile post 184), northwest of Springfield off of U.S. Route 160. From there, the trail runs northwest to Pearl (mile post 178), Harold (mile post 175), and Walnut Grove (mile post 173). Walnut Grove is a small quiet village with at least one country store. The Greene-Polk County Line lies 1 mile north of Walnut Grove, where the trail's smooth surface temporarily ends (mile post 172). In Greene County, the terrain varies from somewhat flat to gently rolling as it follows a blended ridge of landscape with farmland, meadows, and woods.

Cyclists and Horseback riders enjoy the trail (Ozark Greenways).

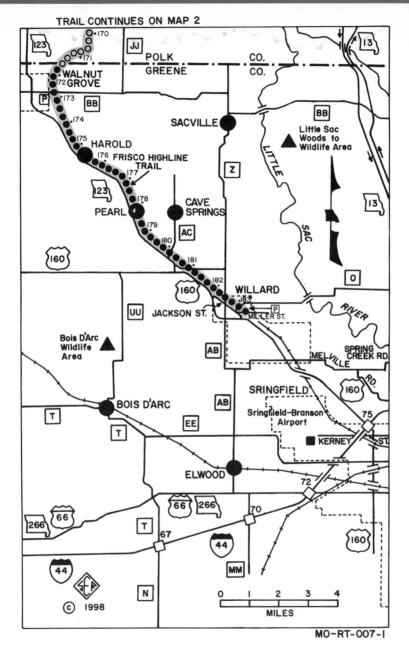

TRAIL CONTINUES ON MAP 2

123
JJ
POLK
GREENE
CO.
CO.
13
WALNUT GROVE
172
P
173
BB
174
175
HAROLD
176 FRISCO HIGHLINE
TRAIL
177
123
178
PEARL
179
180
AC
181
182
160
WILLARD
183
160
UU
JACKSON ST.
MILLER ST.
P
SACVILLE
BB
Little Sac
Woods to
Wildlife Area
Z
LITTLE
SAC
13
O
RIVER
MELVILLE
SPRING
CREEK RD.
RD.
Bois D'Arc
Wildlife
Area
AB
AB
SRINGFIELD
Sringfield-Branson
Airport
160
75
BOIS D'ARC
T
T
EE
KERNEY
ST
ELWOOD
72
66 266
66
266
70
T
67
44
160
44
MM
N
C 1998

0   1   2   3   4
MILES

MO-RT-007-1

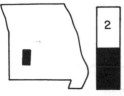

2

FRISCO HIGHLINE TRAIL
(MAP 1)
GREENE & POLK COUNTIES
30.4 MILES (10.0 MILES OPEN)
SURFACE: SMOOTH CRUSHED
GRAVEL

43

In Polk County, the undeveloped section of the Frisco Highline Trail passes through a more picturesque, secluded, wooded, and hilly area. From the Greene-Polk County Line and Walnut Grove, the Frisco Highline Trail runs due north through Graydon Springs (mile post 169), Wishart (mile post 164), and Bolivar (mile post 153). Except for Bolivar, most of the villages along this section of the trail are so small that they don't have any stores. Bolivar, the county seat of Polk County and home to Southwest Baptist University, marks the north end of the Frisco Highline Trail.

The Frisco Highline Trail traverses 16 trestles in Polk County (none in Greene County), including a spectacular railroad bridge that crosses over the Little Sac River between mile posts 166 and 165. Future plans include eventually developing the remaining 20.4 miles of the Frisco Highline Trail through Polk County.

PARKING:
Parking can be found on Miller Street in Willard, and County Route BB in Walnut Grove.

Frisco Highline Trail Trestle #165.8 over the Little Sac River.

FOR MORE INFORMATION:
Ozark Greenways
P.O. Box 50733, Springfield, MO 65805
417-864-2014
http://www.springfield.missouri.org/gov/ozarkgreenways

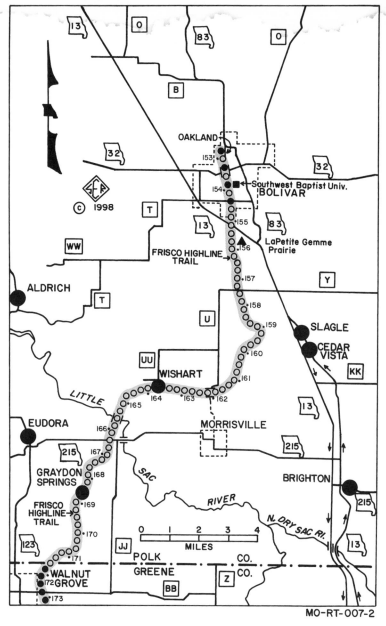

OAKLAND

•153

Southwest Baptist Univ.
•154 **BOLIVAR**

•155

LaPetite Gemme
▲156 Prairie

FRISCO HIGHLINE
TRAIL→

•157

•158

•159 **SLAGLE**

•160 **CEDAR VISTA**

•161

WISHART
•165 164 163 162
•166 **MORRISVILLE**

ALDRICH

EUDORA

215
•167

GRAYDON SPRINGS •168

BRIGHTON

FRISCO
HIGHLINE→ •169
TRAIL

•170

LITTLE

SAC

RIVER

N. DRY SAC RI.

0   1   2   3   4
MILES

123
JJ
•171

**WALNUT
172GROVE**
•173

POLK CO.
GREENE CO.

MO-RT-007-2

FRISCO HIGHLINE TRAIL
2 **(MAP 2)**

1

45

MISSOURI'S MAJOR BIKE TRAILS

WATKINS MILL STATE PARK BIKE PATH

VICINITY: *Lawson*

TRAIL LENGTH: *3.8 miles*

SURFACE: *Asphalt*

TRAIL USE: 🚴 🚵 🥾 🏕 🐎 ⛷ ♿

Originally a plantation owned by Waltus Watkins, the Watkins Mill State Park once consisted of an elegant home and a three-story mill. The mill spun wool into yarn, weaved the yarn into cloth and blankets, and sold those products in a small general store on the mill's first floor. Watkins Woolen Mill operated between 1861 and the late 1880s. In the 1950s, the Watkins Mill Association purchased the property and opened it to the public. In 1963, the association turned the land over to the State of Missouri, which operates it as a state park. Today, visitors to the park can tour the restored Watkins Woolen Mill, the Watkins home, Mount Vernon Church, and Franklin School.

The Watkins Mill State Park Bike Path follows the Williams Creek Lake shoreline. Non-biking activities nearby this 4.5 mile trail include fishing, swimming, boating, camping, and picnicking.

PARKING:
Parking can be found near the north entrance to the park and bike path.

Watkins State Park's restored Watkins Woolen Mill (MO-DNR, Tom Nagel).

FOR MORE INFORMATION:
Missouri Dept. of Natural Resources
Division of Parks and Historic Preservation
P.O. Box 176, Jefferson City, MO 65102
800-334-6946, 816-296-3357 and 816-296-3387

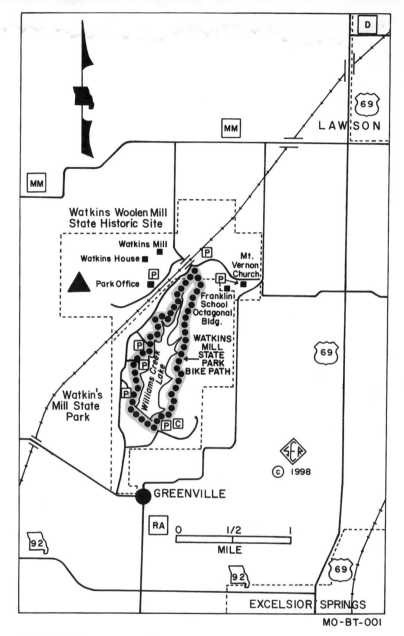

D

69

LAWSON

MM

MM

Watkins Woolen Mill
State Historic Site

Watkins Mill

Watkins House ■

▲ Park Office

P

Mt.
Vernon
Church

P

■ Franklin
School
Octagonal
Bldg.

WATKINS
MILL
STATE
PARK
BIKE PATH

P

P

Watkin's
Mill State
Park

P

P C

Williams Creek Lake

69

Ⓢ·ᶠ·ᴿ
© 1998

GREENVILLE

RA

0   1/2   1
MILE

92

92

69

EXCELSIOR SPRINGS

MO-BT-OOI

WATKINS MILL STATE PARK
BIKE PATH
CLAY COUNTY
3.8 MILES
SURFACE: ASPHALT

ST. JOE STATE PARK BIKE PATH

VICINITY: *De Lassus*

TRAIL LENGTH: *14 miles*

SURFACE: *Asphalt*

TRAIL USE: 🚲 🚴 🚶 📷 🐎 ⛷ ♿

(horses allowed on the 23-mile St. Joe State Park Equestrian Trail)

St. Joe State Park's 8,561 acres make it Missouri's second largest state park. The park is located in southeast Missouri, the nation's "lead belt" where the mineral has been mined since the early 1700s. Around the 1860s, the St. Joe Lead Corporation introduced the diamond-tipped drill, changing the face of hard-rock mining. The St. Joe Lead Corporation operated until 1972 and donated the land to the state in 1976. Today, this area consists of oak and hickory forests and sandflats. A milling complex, once used by the St. Joe Mineral Corporation and curently undergoing resoration, sits at the north end of the park. Non-biking activities available in the park include camping, swimming, fishing, boating, and picnicking.

The fourteen miles of asphalt trail that make up the St. Joe State Park Bike Path can be enjoyed by all non-motorized vehicles. Mountain bikes are permitted on both the park's equestrian trail and bike path.

PARKING:

Parking can be found along Pimville Road near the main park entrance.

St. Joe State Park Bike Path (MO-DNR).

FOR MORE INFORMATION:

Missouri Dept. of Natural Resources
P.O. Box 176, Jefferson City, MO 65102
800-334-6946 and 573-431-1069

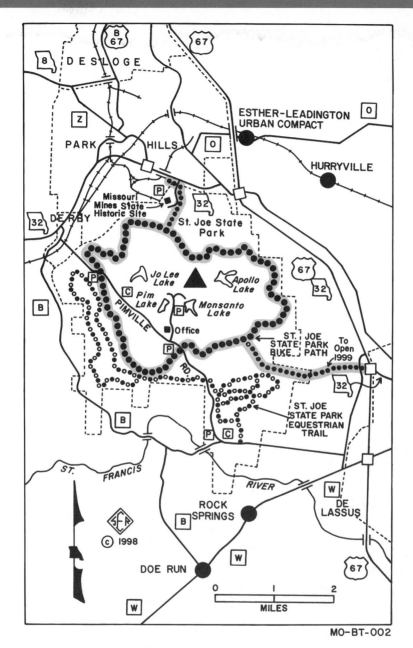

MO-BT-002

ST. JOE STATE PARK BIKE PATH
ST. FRANCOIS COUNTY
14.0 MILES
SURFACE: ASPHALT

FOREST PARK BIKE PATHS

VICINITY: *St. Louis*
TRAIL LENGTH: *7.5 miles*
SURFACE: *Asphalt*
TRAIL USE: 🚲 🛼 🚶 🧺 🐴 ⛷ ♿

St. Louis' Forest Park, first dedicated at a large public ceremony in 1876, consists of 1,371.75 acres, making it one of the largest urban parks in the country. In 1904, the western end of Forest Park hosted the World's Fair. The only permanent building remaining from that event is the Saint Louis Art Museum. Today, Forest Park plays hosts to over 10 million visitors a year. Besides biking, the park offers various activities, including softball, cricket, rugby, tennis, golf, archery, fishing, horseback riding, lacrosse, soccer, ice skating, and roller skating.

The Forest Park Bike Paths run throughout the park, and hilly sections of the asphalt bike path provide cyclists with a good workout. An exercise par course is located along the bike path near the park's north edge between Lindell Boulevard and Grand Drive.

PARKING:
Parking can be found in various areas throughout Forest Park.

Urban Cyclists enjoy the Forest Park Bike Path in St. Louis.

FOR MORE INFORMATION:
Forest Park Forever, Lindell Pavilion
5595 Grand Dr., St. Louis, MO 63112
314-367-7275

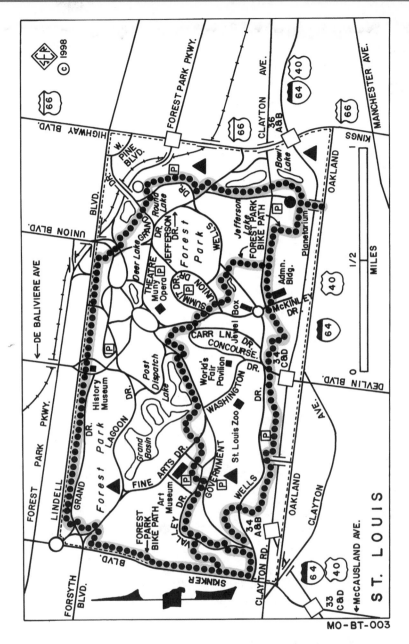

MO-BT-003

FOREST PARK BIKE PATH
CITY OF ST. LOUIS
7.5 MILES
SURFACE: ASPHALT

WESTON BEND STATE PARK BIKE PATH

VICINITY: *Weston Bend*

TRAIL LENGTH: *3 miles*

SURFACE: *Asphalt*

TRAIL USE: 🚴 🚲 🥾 🏕️ 🐎 ⛷️ ♿

The 1,133-acre Weston Bend State Park consists of mud flats left behind by retreating glaciers. The terrain consists of deep ravines and narrow ridges. Much of the surrounding landscape in northwest Missouri originally consisted of prairie and scattered trees; the park is now covered mostly by forest with a few spots of hilltop prairies. The town of Weston, established in 1837 along the Missouri River; found early success growing tobacco and hemp, and by 1858, Weston was the largest hemp port in the world. Even though hemp production has diminished, tobacco still thrives. The park offers plenty of areas for camping and picnicking, including a scenic overlook on a tree-surrounded bluff along the Missouri River that offers a view of Kansas (the overlook is only accessible by those on foot or in wheelchairs).

The Weston Bend State Park Bike Path consists of 3 miles of asphalt that wind through the park, following a small creek through forests before returning along open ridge tops. Riders should excercise caution while maneuvering bicycles along this curvy and hilly trail.

PARKING:

Park near the main park entrance for the Weston Bend Bike Path.

The overlook in Weston Bend State Park (MO-DNR, Tom Nagel).

FOR MORE INFORMATION:

Missouri Dept. of Natural Resources
Weston Bend State Park
16600 Hwy 45 N, P.O. Box 115,Weston, MO 64098
800-334-6946 or 816-640-5443

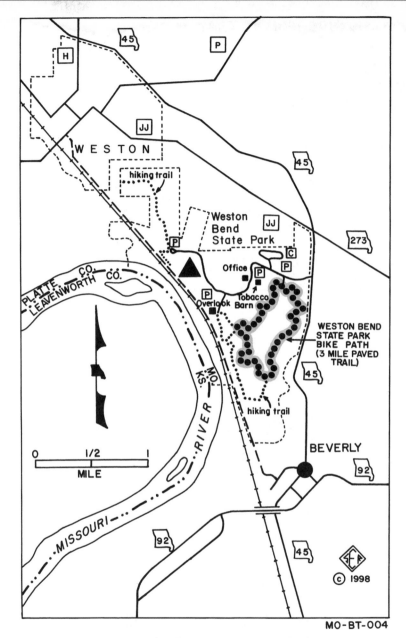

MO-BT-004

WESTON BEND STATE PARK
BIKE PATH
PLATTE COUNTY
3.0 MILES
SURFACE: ASPHALT

ST. LOUIS RIVERFRONT TRAIL

VICINITY: *St. Louis*

TRAIL LENGTH: *10 miles*

SURFACE: *Asphalt*

TRAIL USE: 🚴 🚲 🚶 📷 🐎 ⛷ ♿

The ten-mile St. Louis Riverfront Trail follows the Mississippi River's west bank from the Gateway Arch in Downtown St. Louis to North Riverfront Park. The south end of the trail starts below the Gateway Arch along Sullivan Boulevard and parallels the Mississippi River as it runs north. The trail passes through several of St. Louis' oldest neighborhoods, just north of the Gateway Arch. Scenery is limited for about six miles north of the Arch, as the trail tucks between the Mississippi River on the east side and the active railroad tracks on the west side, leaving very little access for users to enter or leave the trail. Trail users can look across the river between Humbolt and Chambers Roads to see Mosenthein Island, named for a family that once lived on the island. The scenery improves along Riverview Drive as the trail passes through North Riverfront Park. The trail currently ends in North Riverfront Park but future plans include extending it one mile north to the Route 66 Bikeway, providing trail users access across the Mississippi River into Granite City, Illinois.

PARKING:

Parking can be found around the Gateway Arch and North Riverfront Park along Riverview Drive in St. Louis.

The Gateway Arch, St. Louis, MO.

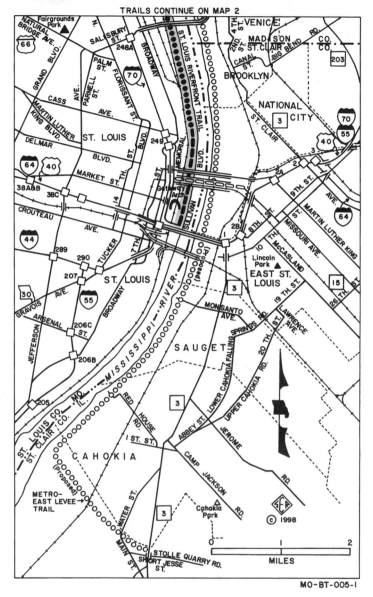

TRAILS CONTINUE ON MAP 2

MO-BT-005-I

ST. LOUIS RIVERFRONT TRAIL
ST. LOUIS COUNTY & CITY OF ST. LOUIS
10.0 MILES; SURFACE: ASPHALT
(MAP I)

ROUTE 66 BIKEWAY

VICINITY: *St. Louis*

TRAIL LENGTH: *1.5 miles*

SURFACE: *Concrete*

TRAIL USE: 🚲 🛹 🚶 🛼 🐎 ⛷ ♿

Also known as the Chain of Rocks Bridge (connecting St. Louis, Missouri, with Granite City, Illinois), the Route 66 Bikeway is a "highways to bikeways" project. At one time, this 1.1-mile bridge was part of legendary U.S. Route 66, which ran between Los Angeles, California, and Chicago, Illinois. The bridge served automobile traffic between 1929 and 1968. In 1967, the nearby Interstate 270 bridge opened to automobile traffic and the U.S. Route 66 bridge was no longer needed. After closing for thirty-two years, the bridge reopened in 1999 as the Route 66 Bikeway. Today, all trail users can enjoy a ride or stroll across the Mississippi River and a wonderful view of the St. Louis City Skyline, whose historic water intake towers look like little medieval castles, and add to the Mississippi River's charm. Eventually, this "highway-bikeway" will connect to both the St. Louis Riverfront Trail in Missouri and the proposed Metro East Bikeway in Illinois.

PARKING:

Parking can be found along Riverview Drive in St. Louis near the Route 66 Bikeway Entrance.

"Highways-to-Bikeways" over the Mississippi River.

FOR MORE INFORMATION:

Trailnet Inc.
3900 Reavis Barracks Rd.
St. Louis, MO 63125
314-416-9930 or 618-874-8554
http://www.trailnet.org

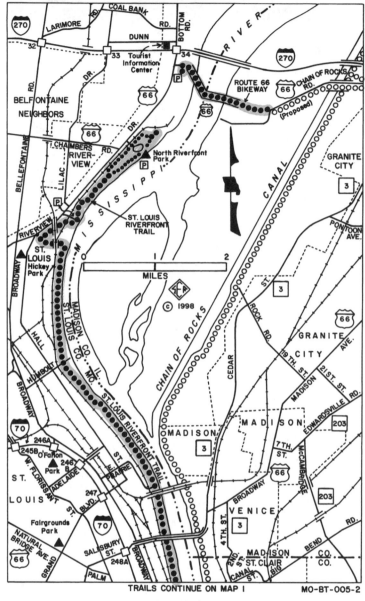

ST. LOUIS RIVERFRONT TRAIL
(MAP 2)

SOUTH/WILSON CREEK

VICINITY: *Springfield*

TRAIL LENGTH: *10 miles (incomplete)*

SURFACE: *Concrete and Smooth Crushed Gravel*

TRAIL USE:

GALLOWAY CREEK

VICINITY: *Springfield*

TRAIL LENGTH: *3 miles*

SURFACE: *Asphalt and Smooth Crushed Gravel*

TRAIL USE:

Springfield, the third largest city in Southwest Missouri's Ozark Region, features a strong business community and a variety of recreational activities. Visitors can enjoy a car safari across the world's largest drive-through wild animal park or explore Fantastic Caverns, the only ride-through cave in North America. Springfield also offers visitors a great zoo and many parks with scenic bike paths. Currently, Springfield has two major bike paths, the South Creek/Wilson Creek Greenway and the Galloway Creek Greenway.

SOUTH CREEK/WILSON CREEK GREENWAY

Most of this trail consists of a 12-foot wide concrete path that meanders through the southern portion of Springfield. When complete, the bike trail will be 10 miles long and connect Meador Park to Wilson's Creek National Battlefield. Currently, a 4.5-mile section follows South Creek from Battlefield Road to Campbell Avenue. Another 1-mile section is open near Roundtree Road, where Wilson Creek Valley offers an abundance of nature.

PARKING:

Parking is found on Roundtree Road, Scenic Avenue, National Avenue, and Meador Park.

GALLOWAY CREEK GREENWAY

Galloway Creek Greenway offers three miles of very scenic biking. The south end of the asphalt trail starts on 181 next to Lake Springfield and meanders north through beautiful woods and meadows, to a three-way trail intersection. To the west, the trail goes to the Springfield Nature Center. Bicyclists and wheel-chair users, however, can only go as far as the railroad tracks—only walkers can continue to the Nature Center. To the north, the smooth, crushed-gravel trail leads to Sequiota Park, paralleling both Galloway Creek and Lone Pine Avenue. Eventually, the trail will extend another 2 miles north to Pershing School.

PARKING:

Parking is found in Sequiota Park, the Springfield Nature Center, and along 181 near Lake Springfield.

FOR MORE INFORMATION:

Ozark Greenways

P.O. Box 50733, Springfield, MO 65805

417-864-2014

http://www.springfield.missouri.org/gov/ozarkgreenways

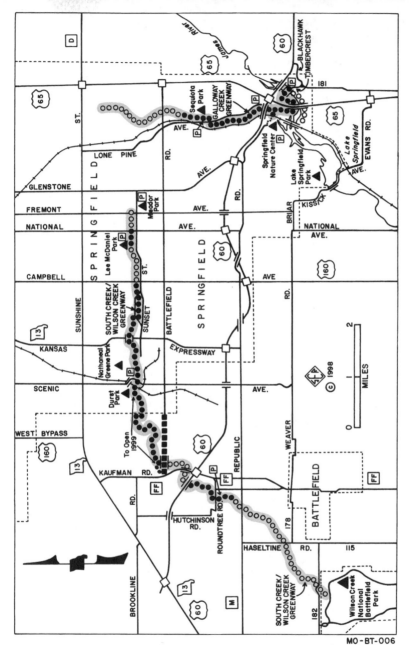

MO-BT-006

SOUTH CREEK/WILSON CREEK GREENWAY
GREENE COUNTY
10.0 MILES (1.0 & 4.5 MILES OPEN)
SURFACE: SMOOTH CRUSHED GRAVEL
GALLOWAY CREEK GREENWAY
GREENE COUNTY ; 3.0 MILES
SURFACE: ASPHALT & SMOOTH CRUSHED GRAVEL

61

BABLER MEMORIAL STATE PARK PATH

VICINITY: *St. Louis*

TRAIL LENGTH: *2 miles*

SURFACE: *Asphalt*

TRAIL USE: 🚲 🛼 🚶 🏕 🏇 ⛷ ♿

(13 miles of separate trails for equestrian use)

Located about 20 miles west of St. Louis, the Babler Memorial State Park was dedicated in 1934, honoring the Dr. Edmund A. Babler, a prominent St. Louis surgeon. The park sits between the hilly Ozarks and the glacial plains and includes Cochran Woods, which consists mainly of beautiful wildflowers and dogwood trees. A visitor's center, a swimming pool, tennis courts, volleyball courts, and basketball courts can be found in the northern end of the park. Picnicking and Campsites with showers are also available. Thirteen separate miles of hiking and horse trails run throughout the entire park. Currently, the 2-mile bike path runs through the southern end of the park. Unfortunately, there is no direct access for trail users from the Babler Memorial State Park to the 235-mile Katy Trail State Park.

PARKING:

Parking can be found within Babler Memorial State Park on the north end of the bike path.

Cyclists stop and enjoy a wooded stretch of the Babler Memorial State Park Bike Path (MO-DNR, David Bradford).

FOR MORE INFORMATION:

Missouri Dept. of Natural Resources
P.O. Box 176, Jefferson City, MO 65102
800-334-6946

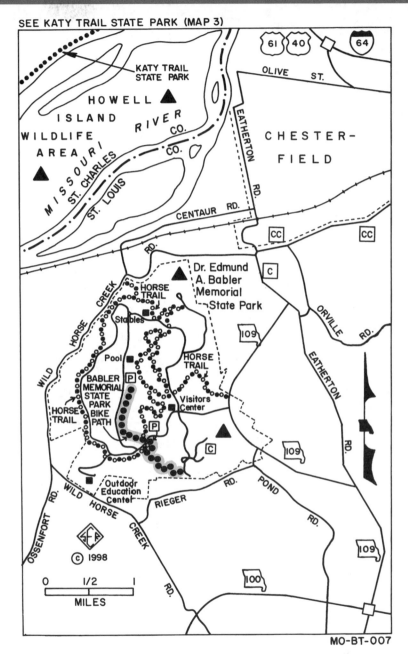

SEE KATY TRAIL STATE PARK (MAP 3)

MO-BT-007

BABLER MEMORIAL STATE PARK BIKE PATH
ST. LOUIS COUNTY
2.0 MILES
SURFACE: ASPHALT

ST. JOSEPH BIKE PATH

VICINITY: *St. Joseph*

TRAIL LENGTH: *9.2 miles*

SURFACE: *Concrete*

TRAIL USE: 🚲 🚵 🚶 🏕 🐎 ⛷ ♿

Robidoux's fur trading post became the City of St. Joseph in 1843. St. Joseph became the county seat of Buchanan County and is the fifth largest city in Missouri. At one time, this industrial city operated eleven railroads with seventy passenger trains arriving and departing each day. Famous for its historical link to the Pony Express and the notorious Jesse James, St. Joseph offers rich historical architecture in urban areas woven with a 26-mile parkway system consisting of scenic landscapes and abundant wooded areas.

The 9.2-mile St. Joseph Bike Path runs in a north-south direction from Krug Park in the north end of the city through Bartlett Park in the city's east end to Hyde Park in the south. The trail closely follows both Northwest and Southwest Parkways, and a section of the route is on Southwest Parkway itself between Commercial Parkway and 14th Street. Future plans include developing an east-west rail-trail from the St. Joseph Bike Path along 28th Street to Riverside Road near US Route 36.

PARKING:

Parking is available near Colby and Northwest Parkways as well as in Krug, Bartlett, and Hyde Parks.

Joyce A. Richardson visits a garden along the St. Joseph Bike Path.

FOR MORE INFORMATION:

Dept. of Public Works and Transportation
1100 Frederick Avenue, Room 204
St. Joseph, Missouri 64501
816-271-5324

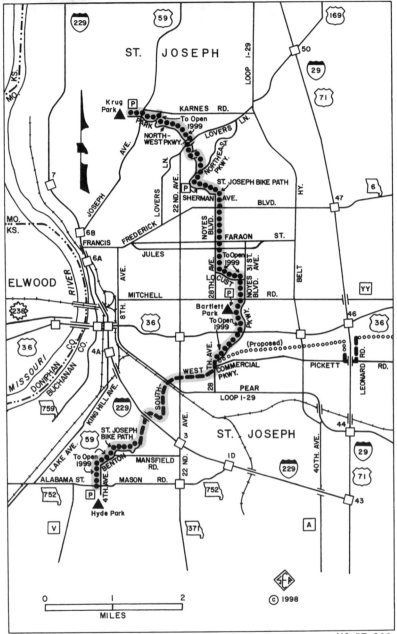

MO-BT-008

ST. JOSEPH BIKE PATH
BUCHANAN COUNTY
9.2 MILES
SURFACE: CONCRETE

MISSOURI'S POTENTIAL RAIL-TRAILS

MISSOURI'S POTENTIAL RAIL-TRAILS

PROPOSED TRAIL NAME	MILES	END POINTS OF TRAIL
Baxter Springs Branch Trail	12	Webb City, MO-Crestline,KS
Chillicothe-Laclede Trail	20	Chillicothe-Laclede
Farmington Trail	8	City of Farmington
Ferguson Jct.-Glen Echo Trail	3	Ferguson Jct.-Glen Echo
Harmony to Preston Trail	11	Harmony-Preston
Kirksville Hike-Bike Trail	3	Kirksville
Marysville Trail	18	Marysville-IA state line
Kansas City-Windsor Trail	40	Kansas City-Windsor
Lee's Summit Trail System	UNKNOWN	City of Lee's Summit
Liberal to Nevada Trail	24	Liberal-Nevada
Owensville-Leeds Junction	UNKNOWN	Owensville-Leeds Junction Trail
St. Joseph Trail System	3	St. Joseph
Sullivan Trail	1	Sullivan
University City Rail-Trail	1	University City
Waco Branch Trail	3	Milepost 139.8-142.9

The tracks that this 1940s-era passenger train ran along, became the predecessor to many of the bike trails that exist today.

For more information on receiving the developments of each trail, contact the Rails-to-Trails Conservancy, 1100 17th. St. NW, 10th. Floor, Washington, DC 20036 or call 202-331-9696.

FURTHER
BICYCLE
ROUTE
INFORMATION

MISSOURI'S PUBLISHED BICYCLE MAPS

MISSOURI (STATEWIDE COVERAGE)

Missouri Bicycle Suitability Map
Missouri Department of Natural Resources, P.O. Box 176,
Jefferson City, MO 65102
800-334-6946 or 800-379-2419 (TDD)
A set of 6 maps. Scale: 1 inch=8 miles.

Watkin Mill State Park Bike Path (MoDNR, Tom Nagel).

MISSOURI BICYCLE SUITABILITY MAP
(A SET OF 6 MAPS)

MISSOURI'S CROSS-STATE BIKE ROUTE MAPS

A. GREAT RIVER BICYCLE ROUTE (#BC-18)

Muscatine, IA to St. Francisville, LA (1335 miles) map
(#BC-1811, Section 1, for Missouri only)
Adventure Cycling Association (formerly Bike Centennial)
P.O. Box 8308, Missoula, MT 59807-8308
800-721-8719
A set of 3 maps for across USA
One map for across Missouri Only
1 inch=4 miles.

B. TRANS AMERICA BICYCLE ROUTE (BIKE ROUTE 76)(#BC-15)

Astoria, OR to Yorktown, VA (4260 miles) map
(#BC-1533, Section 9, for Missouri only)
Adventure Cycling Association (formerly Bike Centennial)
P.O. Box 8308, Missoula, MT 59807-8308
800-721-8719
A set of 12 maps for across USA
One map for across Missouri Only
1 inch=4 miles.

Note: For current prices, contact the appropriate offices. Readers can obtain a free Missouri highway map by writing to the Missouri Department of Transportation, P.O. Box 270, Jefferson City, MO 65102 or calling 888-ASK-MoDOT (888-275-6368).

MISSOURI'S CROSS-STATE BIKE ROUTE MAPS

GREAT RIVERS
BICYCLE ROUTE

MISSOURI

TRANSAMERICA
BICYCLE ROUTE

TRANSAMERICA
BICYCLE ROUTE

GREAT RIVERS
BICYCLE ROUTE

- - - CROSS STATE BIKE ROUTE MAP

BIKE ROUTE LETTER, NUMBER,
OR ABBREVIATION

••••••• RAIL-TRAIL & BIKE TRAIL

© 1998

U.S. RAILS-TO-TRAILS GUIDE BOOKS

U.S. GENERAL

700 Great Rail-Trails: A National Directory of Multi-Use Paths Created from Abandoned Railroads. Rails-to-Trails Conservancy, 1995, 1100 17th. St. NW, 10th. floor, Washington, DC 20036.

A listing of trails for all 50 States. Maps not included.

CALIFORNIA

Rail-Trail Guide to California, Fred Wert, 1995, Infinity Press, P.O. Box 17883, Seattle, WA 98107.

Maps Included.

ILLINOIS

Bicycle Trails of Illinois, 1996, American Bike Trails, 1257 S. Milwaukee Ave., Libertyville, IL 60048.

Maps Included.

IOWA

Bicycle Trails of Iowa, 1996, American Bike Trails, 1257 S. Milwaukee Ave., Libertyville, IL 60048.

Maps Included.

MASSACHUSETTS

Bike Paths of Massachusetts, Stuart Johnstone, 1996, Active Publications, P.O. Box 716, Carlisle, MA 01741.

Maps Included.

MINNESOTA

Biking Minnesota's Rail-Trails, Marlys Mickelson, 1999, Adventure Publications, Inc., P.O. Box 269, Cambridge, MN 55008.

Maps Included.

MISSOURI

Biking Missouri's Rail-Trails, Shawn E. Richardson, 1999, Adventure Publications, Inc., P.O. Box 269, Cambridge, MN 55008.

Maps Included.

NEW JERSEY

24 Great Rail-Trails of New Jersey, Craig Della Penna, 1999, New England Cartographics Inc., P.O. Box 9369, North Amherst, MA 01059.

NEW YORK

Cycling Along the Canals of New York, Louis Russi, 1999, Vitesse Press, 4431 Lehigh Rd, #288, College Park, MD 20740.

Maps Included.

OHIO

Biking Ohio's Rail-Trails, Shawn E. Richardson, 1997, Adventure Publications, Inc., P.O. Box 269, Cambridge, MN 55008.

Maps Included.

PENNSYLVANIA

Pennsylvania's Great Rail-Trails, Rails-to-Trails Conservancy, 1998, RTC, 1100 17th. St. NW, 10th. floor, Washington, DC 20036.

Maps Included.

WASHINGTON STATE

Washington's Rail-Trails, Fred Wert, 1992, The Mountaineers, 1011 SW Klickitat Way, Seattle, WA 98134.

Maps Included.

WEST VIRGINIA

Adventure Guide to West Virginia Rail-Trails, 1998, West Virginia Rails-to-Trails Council, P.O. Box 8889, South Charleston, WV 25303-0889.

Maps Included.

WISCONSIN

Biking Wisconsin's Rail-Trails, Shawn E. Richardson, 1997, Adventure Publications, Inc., P.O. Box 269, Cambridge, MN 55008.

Maps Included.

NEW ENGLAND STATES (CT, MA, ME, NH, RI, AND VT)

Great Rail-Trails of the Northeast, Craig Della Penna, 1995, New England Cartographics Inc., P.O. Box 9369, North Amherst, MA 01059.

Maps Included.

MISSOURI'S TRAILS INDEX AND ADDRESSES

MISSOURI'S CHAMBER OF COMMERCES

State of Missouri	573-634-3511
Bolivar	417-326-4118
Boonville	816-882-2721
Bridgeton	314-739-7010
Chesterfield	314-532-3399, 888-242-4262
Clayton	314-726-3033
Clinton	816-885-8168, 800-222-5251
Columbia	573-874-1132
Farmington	573-756-3615
Ferguson	314-521-6000
Florissant	314-831-3500
Gladstone	816-436-4523
Hermann	573-486-2313
Jefferson City	573-634-3616
Joplin	417-624-4150
Kansas City (North)	816-468-6722
Kansas City (South)	816-942-4333
Kirkwood	314-821-4161, 800-231-4331
Liberty	816-781-5200
Maryland Heights	314-576-6603
Park Hills	573-431-1051
St. Charles	314-946-0633
St. Joseph	816-232-4461
St. Louis (County)	314-889-7663
St. Louis (Regional)	314-231-5555
Sedalia	816-826-2222
Springfield	417-862-5567
University City	314-725-6545
Washington	314-239-2715
Webb City	417-673-1154
Webster Groves	314-962-4142
Windsor	816-647-2318, 816-647-3144

ILLINOIS'S CHAMBERS OF COMMERCES (NEAR ST. LOUIS)

Terry Whaley cruises over the Frisco Greenway Trestle (Terry Whaley).

JOIN THE RAILS-TO-TRAILS CONSERVANCY

RAILS TO TRAILS CONSERVANCY MEMBERSHIP

To join the Rails-to-Trails Conservancy or give a gift member-ship to someone else, simply photocopy and complete this form and mail it along with the appropriate membership fee to the address below.

Name _____

Street _____

City _____

State _____

Zip _____

Phone (include area code):

(home) _____

(work) _____

MEMBERSHIP LEVEL (CHECK THE APPROPRIATE BOX):

☐ Individual Membership $18.00

☐ Family Membership $25.00

☐ Sustaining Membership $35.00

☐ Patron Membership $50.00

☐ Benefactor Membership $100.00

ENCLOSE A CHECK PAYABLE TO:

Rails-to-Trails Conservancy

MAIL THIS FORM TO:

Rails-to-Trails Conservancy
Shipping Department
P.O. Box 295
Federalsburg, MD 21632-0295

To join by using your Mastercard or Visa, call 800-888-7747.

BICYCLE SAFETY

BICYCLE SAFETY

Bicycling offers many rewards, among them a physically fit body and a pleasant means of transportation. But the sport has its hazards, which can lead to serious accidents and injuries. We have provided rules, facts and tips that can help minimize the dangers of bicycling while you're having fun.

CHOOSE THE RIGHT BICYCLE

Adults and children should ride bicycles with frames small enough to be straddled easily with both feet flat on the ground, and with handlebars that can be easily reached with elbows bent. Oversize bikes make it difficult to ride comfortably and maintain control. Likewise, don't buy a large bike for a child to grow into—smaller is safer.

LEARN TO RIDE THE SAFE WAY

When learning to ride a bike, let a little air out of the tires, and practice steering and balancing by "scootering" around with both feet on the ground and the seat as low as possible. The "fly-or-fall" method-where someone runs alongside the bicycle and then lets go-can result in injuries.

Training wheels don't work, since the rider can't learn to balance until the wheels come off. They can be used with a timid rider, but the child still will have to learn to ride without them. Once the rider can balance and pedal (without training wheels), raise the seat so that the rider's leg is almost straight at the bottom of the pedal stroke.

Children seldom appreciate the dangers and hazards of city cycling. Make sure they understand the traffic laws before letting them onto the road.

USE THIS IMPORTANT EQUIPMENT:

Headlight: A working headlight and rear reflector are required for night riding in some states. Side reflectors do not make the rider visible to drivers on cross streets.

Safety seat for children under 40 lbs.: Make sure the seat is mounted firmly over the rear wheel of the bicycle, and does not wobble when going downhill at high speeds. Be sure the child won't slide down when riding. The carrier should also have a device to keep the child's feet from getting into the spokes.

Package rack: Racks are inexpensive, and they let the rider steer with both hands and keep packages out of the spokes.

OBEY TRAFFIC LAWS

Car drivers are used to certain rules of the road, and bicyclists must obey them too. The following rules should be taught to a child as soon as he or she can ride a bicycle:

Make eye contact with a driver before entering or crossing lanes.

Signal and glance over your shoulder before changing lanes.

Watch for openings in the traffic stream and make turns from the appropriate lane.

When riding off-road, be sure you are on a trail that permits bicycles.

Before riding in the road, these rules should be practiced until they become habit and can be performed smoothly. Adults must set good examples-children imitate them regardless of verbal instructions.

BEWARE OF DANGEROUS PRACTICES

Never ride against traffic. Failure to observe this rule causes the majority of car-bicycle collisions. Motorists can't always avoid the maneuvers of a wrong-way rider since the car and bike move toward each other very quickly.

Never make a left turn from the right lane.

Never pass through an intersection at full speed.

Never ignore stop light or stop signs.

Never enter traffic suddenly from a driveway or sidewalk. This rule is particularly important when the rider is a child, who is more difficult for a motorist to see.

Don't wear headphones that make it hard to hear and quickly respond to traffic.

Don't carry passengers on a bike. The only exception is a child under 40 lbs. who is buckled into an approved bike safety seat and wears a helmet as required by law.

Passenger trailers can be safe and fun. Be aware, though, that a trailer makes the bike much longer and requires careful control. Passengers must wear helmets.

FIND SAFE PLACES TO RIDE

Most cities have some bicycle-friendly routes, as well as some high-traffic areas that require skill and experience. It's safest to ride on secondary roads with light traffic. When choosing a route, remember that the wider the lane, the safer the cycling.

GET A BIKE THAT WORKS WITH YOU

Skilled riders who use their bikes often for exercise or transport should consider buying multi-geared bikes, which increase efficiency while minimizing stress on the body. (These bikes may not be appropriate for young or unskilled riders, who may concentrate more on the gears than on the road.) The goal is to keep the pedals turning at a rate of 60-90 RPM. Using the higher gears while pedaling slowly is hard on the knees, and is slower and more tiring than the efficient pedaling.

Have a safe trip!

Reprinted from July 1989 "Mayo Clinic Health Letter" with permission of Mayo Foundation, for Medical Education and Research, Rochester, Minnesota.

BICYCLE HELMETS

"It's as easy as falling off a bicycle." The adage has been around for decades. Unfortunately, it makes light of the potential for tragedy if you should take a serious fall while riding a bicycle.

With an increasing number of people riding bicycles on our streets and highways, the risk of injury-in particular, head injury—continues to rise. Each year, nearly 50,000 bicyclists suffer serious head injuries. According to the most recent statistics, head injuries are the leading cause of death in the approximately 1,300 bicycle-related fatalities that occur annually. To a large extent, these head injuries are preventable.

Wearing a helmet can make a difference. Until recently, advocates of the use of protective headgear for cyclists found their stance lacked scientific support. But wearing protective headgear clearly makes a difference. Recent evidence confirms that a helmet can reduce your risk of serious head and brain injury by almost 90 percent should you be involved in a bicycle accident.

Bicycle riding is an excellent form of aerobic exercise that can benefit your musculoskeletal and cardiovascular systems. Make the investment in a helmet and take the time to put in on each time you ride.

WHAT TO LOOK FOR IN A BICYCLE HELMET:

We endorse these guidelines for bicycle helmets recommended by the American Academy of Pediatrics:

The helmet should meet the voluntary testing standards of one of these two groups: American National Standards Institute (ANSI) OR Snell Memorial Foundation. Look for a sticker on the inside of the helmet.

1) Select the right size. Find one that fits comfortably and doesn't pinch.

2) Buy a helmet with a durable outer shell and a polystyrene liner. Be sure it allows adequate ventilation.

3) Use the adjustable foam pads to ensure a proper fit at the front, back and sides.

4) Adjust the strap for a snug fit. The helmet should cover the top of your forehead and not rock side to side or back and forth with the chain strap in place.

5) Replace your helmet if it is involved in an accident.

A FEW MORE BIKE SAFETY TIPS

By Shawn E. Richardson

RAIL-TRAIL COURTESY AND COMMON SENSE

1. Stay on designated trails.

2. Bicyclists use the right side of the trail (Walkers use the left side of the trail).

3. Bicyclists should only pass slower users on the left side of the trail; use your voice to warn others when you need to pass.

4. Get off to the side of the trail if you need to stop.

5. Bicyclists should yield to all other users.

6. Do not use alcohol or drugs while on the trail.

7. Do not litter.

8. Do not trespass onto adjacent land.

9. Do not wear headphones while using the trail.

EMERGENCY TOOL-KIT

When venturing out on bicycle tours, it is always smart to take along equipment to help make roadside adjustments and repairs. It is not necessary for every member of your group to carry a complete set of equipment, but make sure someone in your group brings along the equipment listed below:

1. Standard or slotted screwdriver.

2. Phillips screwdriver.

3. 6" or 8" adjustable wrench.

4. Small pliers.

5. Spoke adjuster.

6. Tire pressure gauge.

7. Portable tire pump.

8. Spare innertube

9. Tire-changing lugs.

A FEW OTHER THINGS

When embarking on a extended bike ride, it is important to give your bike a pre-ride check. To ensure that your bike is in premium condition, go over the bike's mechanisms, checking for any mechanical problems. It's best to catch these at home, and not when they occur "on the road." If you run into a problem that you can't fix yourself, you should check your local yellow pages for a professional bike mechanic.

When you are planning a longer trip, be sure to consider your own abilities and limitations, as well as those of any companions who may be riding with you. In general, you can ride about three times the length (time-wise) as your average training ride. If you have a regular cycling routine, this is a good basis by which to figure the maximum distance you can handle.

Finally, be aware of the weather. Bring plenty of sunblock for clear days, and rain gear for the rainy ones. Rain can make some rides miserable, in addition to making it difficult to hear other traffic. Winds can blow up sand, and greatly increase the difficulty of a trail.

Katy Trail State Park next to the Missouri River.

ABOUT THE AUTHOR

Shawn E. Richardson has worked as a cartographer for the Ohio Department of Transportation since 1988. He specializes in photogrammetry, the process of creating maps using aerial photography. He received his Bachelor of Science degree in environmental geography with emphasis on cartography from Kentucky's University of Louisville in 1985. A Kentucky native, Shawn has lived in Ohio since 1988. Shawn enjoys bicycle touring, and his excursions can last anywhere from a few hours to several days. Although he has biked back roads through many states, the majority of his touring has been on trails, including Missouri's 235-mile cross-state Katy Trail State Park. He is an active member of the Rails-to-Trails Conservancy and has belonged to the Columbus Outdoor Pursuits, the American Youth Hostels, and to the Louisville Wheelmen. Biking Missouri's Rail-Trails is Shawn's third book. If you have questions or comments for Shawn, you can contact him by writing to him in care of Biking U.S.A.'s Rail-Trails, P.O. Box 284, Hilliard, OH 43026-0284.

Author Shawn E. Richardson and his wife Joyce take a break at a bed & breakfast while traveling across Missouri along the Katy Trail State Park.